LifePOWER

LifePOWER

6 Winning Strategies to
a Life of Purpose, Passion & Power

Veda A. McCoy

iUniverse, Inc.
Bloomington

LifePOWER
6 Winning Strategies to a Life of Purpose, Passion & Power

iUniverse books may be ordered through booksellers or by contacting:

iUniverse
1663 Liberty Drive
Bloomington, IN 47403
www.iuniverse.com
1-800-Authors (1-800-288-4677)

Because of the dynamic nature of the Internet, any Web addresses or links contained in this book
may have changed since publication and may no longer be valid. The views expressed in this work
are solely those of the author and do not necessarily reflect the views of the publisher, and the
publisher hereby disclaims any responsibility for them.

ISBN: 978-1-4502-2571-7 (pbk)
ISBN: 978-1-4502-2572-4 (ebook)

Printed in the United States of America

iUniverse rev. date: 5/13/10

Contents

The Power to "Get a Life"

I want to introduce you to a friend of mine. Perhaps you have met her before. Let's call her *Diligent Delores*. She has all the latest books and cd's on every imaginable topic. Her desk drawers are filled with journals complete with notes from all the various conferences, revivals, retreats, workshops, *WORD*shops, exposés, and roundtables that she has attended. You get the picture? There are files upon files upon files packed with documents outlining visions, dreams, and ideas that promise to be "the one" to take her to the next level. However, Diligent Delores still works at the same job, weighs the same weight, wears the same style of clothes, lives in the same house and neighborhood, exists at the same level of spiritual development, produces on the same plateau of ministry, and enjoys the same diminished sense of peace, joy and fulfillment. As nice as Diligent Delores may be and as filled as she may be with hopes, dreams and potential, she is lacking immensely in the area of MOVEMENT! Delores needs to access the power to move her life FORWARD and to get beyond crying at the altar, falling prostrate after the laying on of hands, and feeling the adrenalin-produced conviction to *really do it this time!*

Diligent Delores is not alone; she is like so many of us. We have the knowledge of our lives as we wish them to be, and we operate with some degree of power. However, we often do not possess the strategies and skills to synchronize our lives with the unlimited power available to us through our relationship with God and our faith in the promises of His Word. This book, *LifePOWER,* discusses how you can strategically get your life on track to produce the dynamic results you are destined to

1

realize. LifePOWER is more than just a slogan. It is more than merely a book. LifePOWER is intended to be a movement – a ***shift*** – to position you to receive passion, purpose and power.

We are promised power in the Word of God.

> *"And what is the exceeding greatness of his power to us-ward who believe, according to the working of his mighty power, which he wrought in Christ, when he raised him from the dead, and set him at his own right hand in the heavenly places."*
>
> *(Ephesians 1:19 & 20)*

According to this scripture the same power that God used to raise Jesus from the dead is not only available to us but *alive within us.* We must BELIEVE that the power is accessible and that we have a divine right to tap into it. The Holy Spirit is in the earth to do more than make us feel exhilarated and overcome with emotion. Running around the church is not the only way to indicate you have tapped into the power of the Holy Spirit. I like to run with the best of them! But after the running is over, I want to know how to live a fruitful life. The Holy Spirit is also more than just a prayer language. Again, I am like Paul and speak with tongues just as much as anybody else. However, the Holy Spirit lives inside of your mind to do more than make you *speak differently.* The Holy Spirit is there to 'lead us and guide us into the truth'. What truth? The truth of what God says about your life. In addition to influencing what comes out of your mouth, the Holy Spirit also enhances what you hear in your spirit. The Holy Spirit will assist you in hearing, processing, and applying the principles of Jesus Christ that will change your life and move you forward to purpose and destiny.

God declared promises over your life before you were even aware that you existed. There are powerful elements of your person residing inside of you, just waiting to be developed and released to impact this world. The life of a believer is intended to be one of action and productivity. You can tap into and demonstrate God's magnificent power to whatever extent your circumstances might require. Furthermore, if you are going to be all that God destined you to be, maximizing the power of the Holy Spirit is a non-negotiable.

So many people are waiting for life to happen to them. They fail to realize that we are sent here to make life happen! Your attitude plays a major role in the unfolding of God's plan in your life. As almighty as God may be – and God is absolutely almighty – you must make the decision to wholeheartedly commit to fulfilling your assignment and realizing your purpose. We have often heard it said that if you fail to plan, then you plan to fail. Accessing God's available power and having it manifest to any degree in your life requires a conscientious, diligent and relentless application of divine principles coupled with practical strategies that must systematically be used in your everyday life. Remember, the word **disciples** is synonymous with the word <u>discipline</u>. Therefore, my purpose for writing this book is to help people go from positions of passivity to postures of power. This book is specifically for the person who is ready to receive something more from a life of faith than the excitement and exuberance from a high praise.

<u>A Faith that Works</u>

Many people have a derogatory view of organized religion because they view it as an opiate for those too weak to deal with life's challenges. In his most recent work entitled, *Have A Little Faith,* Mitch Albom writes that by the time he graduated from high school, he was well-versed in his Jewish faith. Nevertheless, he still pretty much abandoned it as a regular practitioner, because of "a lack of need." He goes on to say that his career as a sportswriter was doing very well and that he really did not need God. *"I was fine. I was healthy. I was making money. I was climbing the ladder. I didn't need to ask God for much, and I figured, as long as I wasn't hurting anyone, God wasn't asking much of me either."* He and God had an "arrangement". In my opinion, Mr. Albom represents the ideology of many "successful" people who feel that if you work hard and do the right thing, you will succeed. In essence, the only people who ask God to make them successful (or happy, fulfilled, etc.), are the people who are too lazy or incompetent to do it themselves. I must admit, I know a lot of church people who give these doubters plenty of evidence for their case. But not all of us want to be this way. Christians sometimes just put their faith in God and expect that "he will do the rest", so they go on about their lives hoping for the best. The reality is, deep down inside most of us know that a relationship with God is supposed to help you do *more with your life,* not give you an escape to help you *settle for less.* In other words, your faith is supposed to work for you. But for many of us, an escape is what our spiritual experience has become. Unfortunately, some of us were conditioned to focus on *the pie in the sky.* Some simply accept that underachieving and struggling through life is the will of God for them. But I am hoping that *LifePOWER* and the strategies taught in this book will help people who may be seeking a more excellent way to live this life of faith. Even the Word of God backs me. The book of James says, "Faith without works is dead." Dead? Dead! If you do not work your faith and allow your faith to produce works (or tangible fruit) for the Kingdom of God, then your faith is not living. Being a believer is about more than fulfilling commitments to "church work"; your entire life should improve as well. As you help to build God a better house and to serve His people who need help, you should be motivated and inspired to improve your living conditions as well. The same goes for education, employment, marriage and family relationships and our emotional/mental well-being. Again, faith should work for you.

Many people in the body of Christ have all of the affects of Christianity and church. They know when to say amen. They do their dance and wave their hands with choreographed precision. But when church is over, they lack the fortitude to become what I call "disciples of their decisions." Some of them do not understand what it means to have a real life, and they seriously need something to do **besides** church! Identities become directly tethered to what we do in church, the status of our spouses, the positions we hold, and what the church membership thinks of us. A significant percentage of Christians lack the ability to access a spiritual life in a practical sense, so when things happen to them outside of the church's four walls, they cannot stand firm. For most people, this condition is somewhat similar to a sleeper terrorist cell, taking up space in their everyday lives until the time of attack. They are often not aware of how ineffective their personal theologies and discipleship efforts are until life hits them hard. To avoid this dilemma, you must be courageous and go on the offense to confront a mindset that says somebody else is responsible for your happiness and progress. This change is what *LifePOWER* is all about.

I believe that we each have a responsibility to participate in the advancement and evolution of our lives. We cannot just dismiss, put off or waitlist God's call for our initiative and action. Therefore, God inspired me to write this book. Once again, *LifePOWER* is designed to ignite passion in the heart of the reader who desires more out of a relationship with God <u>and</u> out of life. The aim of this book is *results*. The focus is not only on results but also how best to achieve them. Readers will receive practical information about how to move their lives in the desired direction and achieve meaningful, lasting results. Sermons and inspirational songs are wonderful, but if we are not willing to do "the work" to improve our lives, then those mountain-top experiences will be short-lived, non-productive, and unfulfilling.

Ruffling a Few Feathers

While this is a book based on Christian beliefs, the Word of God, and godly principles, it is not a quick-fix guide. In fact, *LifePOWER* will challenge the reader in ways that perhaps he or she has not been challenged before. For example, after quoting those powerful scriptures that are heard time and time again over the years, my repeated question to you will be **SO WHAT?!?!?** If you are to be victorious, purpose-driven, destiny-obtaining human beings, you must face the fact that you play a role in your success, or the lack thereof. If you are the type of believer who goes no further than the *name it- claim it/believe it- receive it table,* put this book down now. Give it to a friend! If it was a gift, then please *re-gift it now!* But if you are tired of simply being "full" of potential but not living a life that enjoys what potential can produce, then you've happened upon the right author. If you're finally ready to deliver what you have been *pregnant* with for years, then read on. If you want more than just dreams, then *LifePOWER* is for you. *LifePOWER* is designed to assist you in gaining clarity, direction, effective strategies and productive tactics. My aim is to awaken dreams that have been dormant for years and to aid in mapping out a series of "next steps" to get results. Fear and procrastination do not stand a chance, if you put the principles taught here into action. Real issues that have held you back for years are about to be hijacked and evicted from your life.

My prayer is that after reading this book, you will have the tools necessary to move beyond barriers, oppositions and hindrances to get a life. Get ready for life! Get ready for power! Get ready for *LifePOWER!!* Now, let's begin the journey.

Six LifePOWER Strategies

- Potential
- Purpose
- Parameters
- Planning
- Performing
- Prevailing

Principle #1 – Potential

Potential! An Overrated Attribute

Guess What? Potential Is Overrated! I know that statement might shock you, but it is so true. And here is true story about me to prove it. Some people feel that I am the smartest person they know. I do not say that with hubris or conceit. It simply is the opinion of **some people.** (If you know me and disagree, that is okay!) These people, however, are certain that I have one of the greatest minds they have encountered. For example, my life-long friend, Vikki Johnson often introduces me as "a genius." I think she stretches the truth here a bit; but I'm convinced that *she thinks* I'm pretty smart! If you can find a copy of, *Tales Out of School,* a book written by my high school AP English teacher Dr. Patrick Welch, you'll find that he agrees with what I'm about to tell you. After noting how I boldly told him that I would be in his AP English class in the coming year, he says,

> *"From the beginning, she was one of my favorites. Veda looked you straight in the eye and said exactly what was on her mind. The fact that she was only one of three black students in an AP class of thirty-one didn't seem to faze her a bit. When I asked a question or called for a volunteer, her hand was one of the first to go up. As the year went on her writing improved dramatically . . . and she qualified for college credit on the AP English exam." (Tales Out of School, pp. 80, 82)*

My track and field coach, Bill Yoast – yes, the one from *Remember the Titans* – wrote some of these same things in his book *Remember This Titan,* as well. Coach (as we called him) had this to say about me:

> *"Veda Nicely was one of those Blue Chippers that needed a little extra help. As a hurdler she was as good as it got . . . [s]he was as smart as she was fast and that meant honors classes." (Remember This Titan, p. 134).*

Now, I don't think that I am a genius. I would say that I am gifted intellectually. My mother used to tell me that my brother Jeffrey had me reading before I started nursery school. (Another reason, I'm an advocate for childhood literacy starting at home, BEFORE pre-school. But that's another book!) So, now that you're thinking I am a pompous boaster, let me explain why I opened my book with Principle #1 – Potential. The first thing you must come to understand is that having potential does not mean anything. This fact was true of me as I have sojourned through life, and it might be of you as well. Allow me to explain a bit more. In my life, I have been given many, many, *many* opportunities to capitalize on my "potential" and my God-given gift of a great mind. But I have not always "lived up" to my potential, because I thought my **potential** was somehow my ticket to success. Great things were just supposed to happen for me, just because I was smart. In school, I took honors and AP classes. I took the AP English exam and tested out of freshman-college English. I came from a good home and had a wealth of support. Success should have just fallen into my lap. But it didn't. Potential does not work that way. It didn't for me, and it won't for you.

For example, upon graduating from high school, I was accepted to James Madison University on a partial track scholarship. (Yes, many years – and pounds – ago, I was a track star!) To help me acclimate to college life, I had to enroll in a summer transition program that required me to report mid-summer. I still vividly remember my mother packing up her car and driving me to Harrisburg, Virginia. I recall how she had scrimped and saved so that I could have a television and a few other "luxuries." The people at my church had given me a going away party with lots of fanfare. I was going to college, and this was a big deal. As the United Negro College Fund says, I was not going for just me, but for everybody who loved me and wanted me to succeed. But, guess what? I stayed a week. **One week.** I simply did not want to "change my life" and get used to what I called a mundane environment. I could not get pass the fact that you had to catch a shuttle bus to town. I am sure Harrisburg, VA and the JMU campus are thriving now, but in 1984 it was like a ghost town to me. I called my boyfriend, Marvin (now my husband) and begged him to please come and get me for the weekend, so that I could sing in a concert with a community choir I was a part of at the time. Well, Marvin's red Nova was in need of repairs, and he could not come for another week or two. So, I called around to any and everyone I knew, trying to get a ride back to Alexandria, Virginia! Nobody – and I do mean NOBODY – would come to get me. Not my mother, my sisters, not any of my friends (well, they didn't drive). In hindsight, I realize they were probably trying to help me not blow a great opportunity. But I used this "so-called dilemma" as my excuse to run. I just could not stay at James Madison. And, without talking to anybody, I made up my mind. It was settled. I was going home. And guess what? I did! I packed up everything I had, and I mean *everything* and caught the Greyhound bus back to Alexandria, Virginia. When I arrived at the bus station, I had no money to get home, and my parents did not know I was back in town. So, I hopped in a cab. (I shun now the folly of my ways. What a fool I was!) I figured my parents had to pay the cab and let me in, right? As humorous as it may be now, my actions then were foolish and somewhat tragic. Leaving James Madison at that time aborted my *potential* career as a college athlete. It absolutely removed my *potential* to maybe compete at the Olympic trials for track & field. Who knows what might have happened? It delayed my *potential* to be the first of **eight** children to go directly from high school to college and graduate. It robbed me of the *potential* to meet people from different walks of life and to forge lasting friendships with people who could have expanded my understanding of the world. It pulled right out from under me the *potential* to experience life in ways that had not been thought of by my parents. Although I had the **potential** to do all of these things, my actions caused me to actually realize NONE of them. So, yes, this is the first thing that I want you to understand as you pursue a life filled with real power. POTENTIAL IS OVERRATED!

There are people with a boatload of potential who accomplish considerably less than people whom some might consider as intellectually inferior. Success is realized not only acknowledging the potential you possess, but also by tapping into it and maximizing it to produce results. Unfortunately, many people are too afraid to do the kind of self-work required to actually benefit from their potential. The truth is – **we all have potential, because we are all created in the image of an awesome God!** The God of the Universe is alive in you, and His Holy Spirit is available to you. That is all the potential you need. However, once again, this inarguable fact means nothing if it only exists in the form of POTENTIAL. If you are to ever tap into, maximize and benefit from all of the great potential that lies within you, you will have to do more than just possess the potential. You must use strategic tools to bring out the best in you.

The word potential means *existing in possibility, the inherent capacity for coming into being, likely and expected to be or become.* In the case of electrical power, the word means *electric potential, the difference in electric charge between two points in a circuit.* To translate the latter meaning into a context pertaining to this discussion, "potential" is the difference between two very important points. Point #1 is what God says about us. Point #2 is what we say about ourselves. To put it another way, potential indicates the space (or choices made and actions taken) between **receiving a word of promise** and following through with the discipline, faith and strength of character necessary to **act upon the word of promise**. That my friend is how you get the power to lead the life of your dreams. In a nutshell, that is *LifePOWER!*

Avoid the tendency that allows that space between these two points to become a place of the *unfulfilled capacity* described above. Be alive in that place. Be focused in that place. Live by godly principles and be driven by clearly-defined goals in that place. This place – the potential within us – is the place where we are catapulted from wishing and wanting to realization and fulfillment. The choice is yours. Fulfilled dreams, fulfilled realities, and fulfilled passions are all possible, but they are not guaranteed. Remember, the **same power that raised Christ from the dead lives in you and is available to you** (Ephesians 3:20). However, if you fail to tap into it, having it does not matter much.

Because, UNTAPPED potential is the same as UNUSED POWER. Both are wasted!

So, now there are still questions. *How do you close in the distance between what is spoken and what you realize? How do you become examples of potential maximized and not simply potential conceptualized?*

I admit that these are not easy questions. And, as I commented before, many people would rather just give God "a praise" and standby while they "watch God work it out!" As I stated earlier, I love to shout and dance, too. I even run every now and then. But as I have grown in my faith and matured in my understanding of spiritual things, I have come to believe that the greatest "praise" we can give God is to simply show up on the stage of our lives and perform to our greatest ability. This is how we bring glory to the name of our God – by being a *living epistle* of God's goodness that people can read without ever opening a Bible. I believe that the angels will ring out melodious hallelujahs and shout to the Lord our God that He's done it again, if you and I can release our unique potentials to show forth God's splendor.

Know Who You Are

So, how does one cross the bridge from untapped power to limitless potential? What can be done? What does the Word of God say about us and our potential? The answer is simple. **You must know who you are!** You must understand that who you really are and what truly matters about you NEVER CHANGES.

> *Genesis 1:27 says, "So God created man in God's image; in the image of God created God him; male and female created God them.*

> *Psalm 8:4-6 says, "What is man that thought art mindful of him and the son of man that thou visit him. For thou has made him a little lower than the angels, and has crowned him with glory and honor. Thou made him to have dominion over the works of thy hands; though has put all things under his feet:"*

Your image of yourself and the essence of your value must be based on the word of God. Not your family background. Not where you live.

Not your socio-economical status. Not the bad things that may have happened in your past. When you know your created potential, no negative circumstance can stop you. Your POTENTIAL comes about as a result of WHO YOU ARE as a child of God. When you look in the mirror, you must recondition your mind to see "God's image" looking back at you. Because, that is what God sees when He looks at you. God sees His creation. God sees His power. God sees His compassion. God sees His knowledge. God sees Himself. And when you see yourself from this perspective, you realize that within YOU is a potency that can change your life for the better and have an impact on this world that will never die. When you understand that you are created in the image of God – a little lower than the angels themselves – you realize that there is nothing lacking *in* you and nothing lacking *about* you. You shake off the mentality that says you should sit back and wait for God to change and improve your life, because you have the revelation. The truth is that God is waiting on us to assume our divine identity and maximize the potential within us. Your thinking will change when you understand these truths. You become motivated to literally call *heaven down to earth* and to *establish the Kingdom of God in the earth*. This what the scripture means in *Matthew 6:10, "Let Your Kingdom come, let your will be done on earth as it is in heaven."*

Be God's Earth Agent

You are God's agent in the earth. You have the capability to impact this world and turn the hearts and minds of people towards God, with your God-given potential. Once you understand this, you aim to "max out" on who you are and what you can offer. For years, many of us maxed out our credit cards. We pushed them to the limit, often standing at the checkout register *praying* that the transaction would go through. The same should be true of the spirit. Max out your potential. Push yourself. Test the limits and boundaries that surround your life. Dig a little deeper. Go beyond scratching the service. When you leave an assignment, make sure there is nothing else you could do or give to make it great. I am confident that as we empty ourselves out and pour our *potential* out into the world, God will be faithful to fill us up again.

Principle #2 – Purpose
NOT Just Another Book on Purpose!

I promised myself that I simply would not buy another book on "purpose." So when I was inspired to write one I thought, "Now why would I do that, since if I saw the book in the store I probably wouldn't buy it?" Life is simply too short to engage in activities that you do not completely and whole-heartedly believe in. But as I prayed over the assignment, I realized that I am not to write just another book on purpose. My intent is to do more than simply awaken some sense of *why* you are here and *how to figure out your purpose*. I want you, the reader, to experience more than just an urgency of *what your purpose is.* My assignment is to bring to a halt the continued participation in repetitious, non-productive and unfulfilling life patterns that often cloud purpose or hinder it altogether. I'm sure that you will agree with me when I say that sometimes figuring out how to accomplish the purpose, once it is revealed, is completely overwhelming. Sometimes it is easier to just put it off year after year after year. The sensational, emotional experiences we have at church must be followed and reinforced by practical instructions on how to simply "do life." And I've come to know that **life is a** trip! It is not only a "trip" that takes you on a journey going from experience to experience, but it is also the kind of "trip" that will sometimes make you forget your name and address! Life can throw so many curve balls at one time, that you will think you are living in a dream – or maybe it is a nightmare! Life should come with a warning – *Professionals Only!* And only those who pack their bags, hit the road and stay with it for the long haul will reap the benefits of a fulfilling life. And living life – or what I call *doing life* – is a skill understood by very few people and mastered by even fewer. This explains the number of people who may know what their purpose is, but they cannot seem to find a way to move forward in its direction. No, I do not want to just write a book about purpose. I want to say more about purpose than just why you are here. I want examine purpose as a strategy and a tactic used to produce the POWER you need to transform your life.

What is Purpose Really About?

Purpose is not about being famous or significant in the eyes of others. Purpose is about what you do every day. Purpose is about consistency. Purpose is the tenacity to stay the course. Purpose is the thing that fuels your discipline as you move towards your destiny. Purpose is the filter through which you view your life. Purpose is how you *do life* and how you make sure that your *life gets done!* Here are a few things I have learned about purpose.

You Are Born With a Purpose

You need a particular "mind set" – a mentality and an intellectual disposition – to transform the way you view life and the manner in which you behave. In order to "do life" according to your purpose, you must think a certain way. This thinking begins with understanding the power of purpose. To begin, you are born with a purpose.

> *"Before I shaped you in the womb, I knew all about you.*
> *Before you saw the light of day, I had holy plans for you"*
> *(Jeremiah 1:5 – MSG).*

The plan for your life did not begin when your parents met. It did not even begin when they fell in love. The plan for your life did not start at your conception or on the day you were born. It began in eternity. Your being born was just God taking advantage of another opportunity to show off. Show off what? Well, His marvelous mind of course! I used to always say, *"God is about to show the world what he had in mind when he spoke my name in eternity!"* That was my way of staying focused on my future and my purpose in life. I was reminding myself, that in spite of how bad my circumstances might be and regardless of how messed up I might have been at that moment, God had ***already planned*** great things for me. I just had to get it in gear and get with The Program! The same is true for you. You can view your purpose as a beautiful vase that sits on a shelf collecting dust. Or you can take it down, let it get dirty, maybe even a little chipped and trust that God will provide for, protect and perfect it along the way.

An Example of Purpose on Target

Another example of a person who understood purpose as a call to action was Esther. The Bible says that when she became queen, she was called into the kingdom for "such a time as". All of the pampering and special treatment that Esther received while being considered as the next queen for King Ahasureus was preparing her for a specific moment of purpose. I am certain that while she was being treated so well, she had little idea that she would soon face a situation that might end in her death. But once Mordecai revealed her purpose, even in the face of monumental peril, Esther agreed to obey God, and she moved forward. She saw all of the events in her life as leading her to and preparing her for this very moment. This included being an orphan, looking different from the other Jews, being cared for by Mordecai, finding favor with the palace, and even being a favorite of the King. It all was a part of God's plan to set Esther up to operate in her purpose. And Esther immediately went into action to fulfill her assignment. Look at her response to Mordecai.

> *Go, gather together all the Jews that are present in Shu'shan,*
> *and fast ye for me, and neither eat nor drink three days,*
> *night or day: I also and my maidens will fast likewise; and*
> *so will I go in unto the king, which is not according to the*
> *law: and if I perish, I perish. (Esther 4:16)*

Walking in purpose is not an easy thing. Nothing in life is clear cut or easy, especially fulfilling destiny and walking in purpose. Walking in purpose requires that you be strategic and strong. Like Esther, you must be willing to fight for the things that are important to you. Esther's fight was not physical or natural; it was spiritual. And she used her spiritual wit to plan and implement her strategy. After accepting that you were born with a divine assignment, you must put your eyes on doing it and declare that nothing will stop you. Along with the resolve and commitment comes the knowledge that there *will* definitely be a fight. So, you must be prepared for it! Get yourself a support system. Just like boxers, people of purpose need a trainer and a staff. Allow God to lead you to the right team of a pastor, mentors, friends, prayer partners, and ministry friends. And when the enemy comes against you and perhaps knocks you down, you can go to your ring-side corner. With your support system in your corner, you can get the help and attention that you need. When you feel yourself getting weary, do not give up on your purpose. That is *NOT* the answer!

> *Hebrews 10:35, 38 say, "So do not give up your hope which will be greatly rewarded. But the upright man will be living by his faith; and if he goes back, [God] has no pleasure in him."*

Our faithfulness not only gets us the reward, but our faithfulness also brings pleasure to God! It allows God's plan and purpose for our lives to be totally brought to pass. So, let your purpose be your driving force to get you up out of complacency and past despair. When you need renewal, run fast to your corner, and get your water – which is the presence of God and the comfort of the Holy Spirit. Let the "training team" wipe the sweat from your forehead and the tears from your eyes. Let them ask you if you are ready to give up, throw in the towel and let the devil win! And make sure your answer is No! Because, *greater is the God in you and the enemy in the world!* Because, as they say in show business, the show must go on. And the same is true for you; *your purpose must go on!* And when you come out of your corner, come out swinging with renewed strength. Here are a few additional strategies for getting on track with your purpose.

How to Walk in Your Purpose Successfully

Seek Diligently for Your Purpose

Unfortunately, purpose does not always walk up to your front door and knock to introduce itself. Rarely does purpose move in next door and become your new neighbor. You must seek within yourself for what your purpose is and for exactly how you should direct your focus. Then, diligently focus on what purpose *really is.* Sometimes, pursuing purpose mistakenly leads to focusing on seeking popularity, position, prestige and power. Proper focus becomes diverted and all of your energies are spent on doing whatever it takes to become the next most-celebrated person. If you belong to the church community, it might be a singer, evangelist, prophet or bishop. However, titles and public recognition can never give the sense of fulfillment and peace that TRUE PURPOSE does. Focusing on being rich, secure, welcomed and admired is the same as doing everything to treat the symptoms of an illness but ignoring the disease itself.

> *Proverbs 18:16 says, "A man's gift makes room for him, and brings him before great men."*

In this scripture, use the word "purpose" in place of the word "gift." This means that your *purpose* will create a place for you in just the right place. When you seek within for your purpose and agree by faith to pursue it wholeheartedly, you will walk right into the divine will for your life. And with divine will comes divine provision. God's provision has a way to bring everything together. However, things do not come together to make you rich and famous. Rather, they come together to make you successful at fulfilling your specific assignment. So, as you diligently seek your purpose, be careful to always remember that glamour does not equal happiness. What is a blessing to one may very well be a disaster to someone else. All of other ladies who competed to be queen were probably jealous of Esther, right up until the time that the purpose of her selection was revealed! It is easy to look at what other people are doing in the areas of ministry, career, family, and business. All of the glitz and the perks can seem so alluring. What is not readily seen is what it cost the person to get there. And you definitely do not know what is required of a person to maintain it. And, if you are not in the right *place of purpose,* then you will not have the flow of *grace for YOUR purpose.* Only God knows what you were sent here to do. And only God can give you the tools, resources, assistance and perseverance you need to be successful. So ask God! Fast, pray, consecrate, get in the Word of God. Do whatever it takes. Be committed to connecting with God's purpose for your life.

Esther, once again, provides a tremendous example of full discovery. Once Esther discovered that her place in the palace was indeed for more than enjoying the pleasures of being queen, she was diligently and relentlessly obedient. And, Esther was also wise. She told Mordecai to call a fast and start praying. She made up her mind to go see the king, even though it meant she was treading on dangerous territory. She knew that she needed a strategy. She knew that her plan must begin with finding out exactly what she was supposed to do and how she was supposed to do it. Esther was clear on what was her purpose, and she was successful in saving the Jews.

Lastly, as you diligently seek your purpose, also remember to practice patience. When you are given a glimpse of what you are called to do, sometimes there is a temptation to move forward hastily. Preparation, clarity and direction are bypassed for the immediacy of the moment. Right away, there are business cards with a new position on them. Next, is the demand that everyone start using a new title that represents the respect that the position deserves. However, you must understand that purpose is just as much a means to an end as it is the end itself. There is more learned about purpose in the process of fulfilling it than you could ever learn just by jumping to the end result. The point of your purpose is not just to be called by a title. Your purpose is to do the work that comes with the title, to serve people through the work that grows out of your calling. In other words, sometimes the true miracle of purpose is the journey we take to get there. The *process* is also a part of the purpose, and you must be prepared to trust the process of your purpose as it unfolds. If you are faithful to your divine purpose, recognition may or may not come. However, most people who have the right focus and are busy doing their life's work, are not appeased by titles, recognition and popularity when they arrive.

Had Esther marched into the King's quarters without patience, she might have been executed for a violation of the law. Her premature death would have prevented her from fulfilling her purpose of saving the Jews from annihilation. When Esther went in to see the King, even though he welcomed her, she did not tell him everything. Because Esther exercised patience, she was able to carry out her plan. Her patience led to the divine strategy that she was given which allowed her to fulfill her purpose.

> *"Then said the king unto her, What wilt thou, Queen Esther? And what is they request? It shall be even given thee to the half of the kingdom. And Esther answered, "If it seem good unto the king, let the king and Haman come this day unto the banquet that I have prepared for him." Then the king said, "Cause Haman to make haste, that he may do as Esther hath said. So the king and Haman came to the banquet that Esther had prepared." (Esther 5:3-5)*

Esther could have very well blurted to the King what her plight was, but that apparently was not what she was guided to do. As a result of her patience, she was led to fast and pray. During this period of consecration Esther received strategic insight. As you move forward in diligently seeking your purpose, understand that the journey will require patience. Patience can save you a ton of trouble on the road to destiny. Patience allows you to trust God. God can see down the road and around the corner. Your true purpose can only be carried out if you are willing to submit to the process – and this requires patience. Because, in actuality, *the purpose itself belongs to God!* It does not belong to us. This is a reason to rejoice because the fact that you and your purpose belong to God, means that helping you to succeed is also God's responsibility. You are not in this alone; the power of God is right there ready to help you. I rejoice about this personally, because my "God job" – as *wife, mother, family member, prophet, teacher, pastor, preacher, teacher, singer, counselor, leader, mentor, writer, administrator, and "other duties as required"* – is too much for me to handle by myself! But somehow, when I am focused, disciplined, obedient and diligent, I am successful at completing my various assignments. And as long as I give God the glory when things are going well, I can also give God the burden of giving me everything I need to bring the visions, plans and dreams that He has given me to pass. My job is to find out *what* and to get strategies of *how,* and to *move into action by faith.* The rest is on God! But you can only have this kind of assurance and security when you have gotten your direction straight from God as a result of diligently seeking out your purpose.

Make Everyday A Purpose Day

Jesus instructed his disciples to pray after this manner: *"Give us this day, our daily bread."* This prayer format is also an excellent life strategy!

Too often we focus on everything except today – tomorrow, yesterday, other people, and situations. What we must remember is that we cannot change the past, and tomorrow is not promised. However, you can make today count. When you wake up in the morning, tell yourself, "I will walk in my purpose ***today!***" Take Jesus' advice and take it one day at a time. For he said, *"Give us this day, our DAILY bread."* Focus on what you can accomplish and control today. Yes, it is important to have goals and objectives. However, the only time you have to get something done is right now! You can *plan* for tomorrow, but you can only *act upon a plan* today! Let tomorrow take care of tomorrow. Sometimes, purpose can be intimidating as it is such a "big picture". People avoid the daunting task of getting it "all done", because the idea of all it will entail to be successful is too much to comprehend. People often forget that you accomplish things of purpose the same way that one might eat an elephant – one bite at a time! If you can string together a series of "days" with efforts of moving towards purpose, before you know it you will be standing right at the door of greatness.

If you have decided to walk in purpose, you must refuse to be plagued by the dilemmas of the past. *Lamentations 3:22 says, "It is of the Lord's mercies that we are not consumed, for they are* <u>*new every morning*</u>*."* Remember that there is nothing that can happen in this day, that the mercies of God cannot get you through. Forget about yesterday! It cannot be changed. Make it your daily goal to use all of each day's mercy. Stretch yourself. Go to the edge of your limitations and possibilities. Put God to the test of His Word and promises each and every day. Challenge your faith. Do not waste today's mercy on just repenting and rehashing things of your flesh. You are more than your habits, idiosyncrasies and faults! Mercy is good for these, yes, but mercy is also good for helping us to stand in the face of what seems to be impossible, impassable, and unrealistic. Mercy can give you a "nevertheless" mentality that says, "If God has led me to this assignment and purpose, then the mercy and grace of God can keep me and help me to be successful!"

Esther did not anguish over the fact that her yesterdays consisted of days of pampering, gold thread in her hair and sweet perfume. Neither did she worry about what would happen *after* she went to see the King. She simply made *each day* count. Her mind was made up that regardless of what might happen she was determined to see the king. Her yesterdays were gone, and she might never be pampered again. Tomorrow would have to take care of itself, and if it brought about her death – so be it. On *that day,* her purpose and assignment were to intervene on behalf of her people and to ultimately save them. And by making the day count, she accomplished her goals. Esther's model is one to be followed.

Make Everything In Your Life Tie Into Your Purpose

Every person, place and thing in your life must coincide with God's plan for you. Otherwise, you are wasting their time and yours as well. God's purpose for your life is the road map that every element of your life must follow. Your purpose is the standard to which every component of your existence must eventually conform. In this regard, you must be hard-nosed, uncompromising and diligent. Be careful not to allow people to merely take up space in your life. Make sure that they have a current, relevant reason for being there. Perhaps they have always been there. Maybe at one time, they did you a huge favor. It could be that at one point, they shared the same values, goals and life's ambitions as you. Or, the case may be that, in the past, they really needed you. While these and other truths might be important, what really matters is what purpose these people serve in your life today.

I am one of the most loyal people that you can ever meet. Sometimes, I am loyal to a fault. I have relationships that date back decades, and these people will always be a part of my life and be held dear to my heart. If they ever need me, I am there. I will never betray their confidence, nor sabotage any of their success. However, that does not mean that they are connected to my purpose in life today. Nor does it mean that they are a part of my everyday life. This is a very touchy subject to some people, especially for people who are not absolutely confident of their identity. People who lack confidence feel they need everybody. People who are not sure of their identity feel obligated to everyone. There are no lines of delineation that say, yes we can chat from time to time, we can even exchange an email here or there, or possibly do lunch to catch up on things. But for a person to actually be in your life – up close and personally – means that they understand who you are and what you are purposed and destined to be. You become connected on a plane where common, casual relationships do not always intersect. A purpose relationship is one of exchange, reciprocity and equal responsibility.

The power to choose and define who or what is directly (or indirectly) connected to you belongs exclusively to you. You must decide what role each person in your life will play. People can add to your life, or they can take away from it. Unfavorable situations can teach you lessons, or they can merely be experiences that will likely happen again. Take back the control of your life. You are the captain of your ship. The ship of your life is sailing now as you read this book. It is moving upon the waters of time, being driven by your decisions, impacted by your circumstances and qualified by your outcomes. Take a minute and ask yourself these simple, but deeply reflective questions. Take your time, be honest with yourself and make particular note of your responses. *Are you at the helm of your life? Or are you simply going along for the ride?*

Too often we relinquish the control of our lives to chance and happenstance. You cannot control people or their actions; however, you can control whether or not their actions will impact you. Recently, God inspired me with this revelation. *Access to your life is access to your anointing and all that is good about you.* The revelation was followed by a divine mandate. *Stop bartering with your anointing. Stop exchanging access to your life for the filling of emotional and psychological needs which only God Himself can fill. Stop allowing people access to your life to please only them and to accomplish only their objectives. Relationships are intended to be reciprocal, even exchanges of give and take.* And, as you move through life, everybody in your life moves with you. Whatever you do, wherever you go and whenever you represent yourself you do not stand alone. Everyone in your life stands with you. The people in your life say something about you and what you think about yourself. Believe it or not, the people who attend special events in your life – even your funeral – can say more about you that you could every say yourself. Open the door to your life very, very carefully.

Once again, I offer Esther as an example. Esther made all of her maids and servants fast with her. When she was trying to figure out a plan and a strategy, she made sure that everyone near her was contributing to her <u>current purpose</u>. Whether they believed in Jehovah or not, Esther required that they fast with her, so that she could get clarity for what she was about to do.

*"Go gather together all the Jews that are present in Shushan,
and fast ye for me . . . I also and my maidens will fast
likewise" (Esther 4:16).*

Again, people with the privilege of being close to you must understand
who you are, where you are going and what your assignment is when
you get there. They must be dependable, trustworthy and committed
to your purpose. In addition, they must have a strong sense of purpose
and direction for their own lives. Direction and purpose are important,
because when people do not know who they are several things can
happen. They might be threatened by your progress. They might rely
on you for their identity. Or, they may feel that they are eternally linked
to you and where you are going. The latter mentality will make them
needy and selfish. They will not want other people to come and go
in your life. When you begin to grow, mature and flourish, they feel
slighted as if you are leaving them, and that they no longer matter to
you. I call this "claiming ownership." When people claim ownership
of you, as soon as you make a decision that does not include them, you
have somehow wronged them. People in your life must understand that
you are a person of purpose, and that you will move as you are led to
move. You belong to God and God alone.

Also, when people do not understand what it means to live a life
of purpose, they will bail out on your just when you need them the
most. To engage in the process of life from the perspective that you
will fulfill your destiny and walk in your purpose is not an easy task.
Times will become difficult. Unfavorable decisions will have to be
made. Circumstances and situations will arise for which you will have
no explanation except to say that you are standing on the promises of
God. If people are with you for the wrong reason or if they are unsure
of themselves, they will not render to your life and your process what
close relationships are intended to bring. Sometimes, people in your life
must have the courage to tell you when you are wrong. They must be
God's mouthpieces of warning that your actions will bring about self-
destruction. Only people who truly love you and want you to please
God – even if it means you being displeased with them – are able to be
there for you in times like these.

Having a life of power means that purpose is at the beginning, the
middle and the end of everything you do. No matter where you may

be at any given moment, you mirror the actions of Esther who truly believed, *"I have been brought to the Kingdom for such a time as this."* You live under a different kind of mandate. There is a resolve that even if some aspects of your life must fall away and perish, pleasing God and fulfilling your divine purpose must take preeminence. And, it is only through utter commitment to your purpose that you accomplish great and mighty things! Identifying, accepting, pursuing and walking in purpose are fundamental principles to having *LifePOWER!*

Principle #3 – Parameters
Establish Your Boundaries and Stick With Them!

I like to think of boundaries as the gates we place around our lives, to keep our life energy from escaping and being wasted. The same that way energy can escape through poorly insulated windows and drafty doors, God's power can *seep* out of our lives into wasteful, unproductive places. Those places usually take the form of unhealthy, meaningless relationships. Many of the relationships in our lives are just like poorly insulated windows. They are losing energy fast and running up sky-high utility bills. The only difference is we do not pay this utility bill with money, we pay it with our very life in the form of energy, healthy, strength, and attention. Unfortunately, we are often so involved in the happenings of these relationships, that we miss the glaring reality that they are completely out of whack. They lack the boundaries to keep them in place, and they need clearly defined lines of demarcation that say where they start, where they end, what comes into them and what goes out from them.

Do You Have An Energy Conservation Problem?

Is your life draining you? Do you feel unfulfilled, despite the fact that you are busy, busy, all of the time? Perhaps you have an energy conservation problem. There are several reasons that energy conservation problems go unnoticed by homeowners. Residents cannot see the air flowing in and out of window crevices and door posts. Therefore, they think that the boundaries of the home are doing their job effectively. But when a ridiculously high electric bill arrives in the mail, the culprit is exposed. Or, maybe the cold drafts that keep drifting in and out make it impossible to ignore the truth. There is indeed a problem somewhere! The same can be true of you. You have power seeping and leaking out of your life all of the time. The quality of your spiritual, financial, emotional, psychological and physical well being is highly impacted by how well you manage your boundaries. And, as in the case with energy trickling out of homes, you can be unaware that an energy crisis is underway. Nevertheless, you do experience the symptoms of the condition in the form of burn-out, depleted joy, manufactured praise, inconsistent faith, stagnant spiritual development and underachieving ministries. Failure to properly insulate your life with boundaries can result in your spiritual power and supernatural energy going everywhere, except where they are needed the most.

Power leaks can be caused by many things. Poor mental attitudes, self-destructive behaviors, and hidden bitterness harbored are just a few that can drain us dry of God's power. Sometimes, the power supply is wasted because of the people in a person's life. This reality is often the hardest for people to face, because we tend to be loyal, even to a fault, to the people with whom we have history. We remain consistently committed to people, even if we know that doing so is not beneficial, and perhaps may even be detrimental, to us.

Who Are You Today?

People come into your lives to add, subtract or multiply. Furthermore, people must also *grow with you,* as you continue along your journey towards spiritual and personal wholeness. You are not the exact same person you were 10 to 15 years ago. Hopefully, in as few as even the last five years, you have progressed, matured and evolved. Imagine someone who knew you as a teenager expecting you play the same pranks and games you did back then. Let me share a story with you. When I was a little girl, I had a friend named, Lisa Lipscomb. The Lipscomb's lived across the street from us; my mother and Mrs. Lipscomb were very good friends. Lisa was one month older that I, and we literally grew up together and remain friends to this day. I've known Lisa as long as I have known myself. I recall this one game that we played all the time. We would go to a nearby community called Jefferson Village, and we would knock on our neighbors' doors and run before they opened them. Sometimes we would knock on the same door three or four times in a row. I laugh now when I think of how much fun that was. I am telling you the truth; we would play for hours and laugh until we could hardly stand. Mr. Meekins, the property manager, chased us out of that complex on so many occasions. I later became somewhat of a track star, no doubt in part because I learned to run very fast to get away. It was sheer delight – *to a 10 year old little girl!!!*

Later, Lisa joined the same church as I and became a part of the security ministry. As an employee with the sheriff's office, people now knew Lisa to be a responsible, dependable and conscientious young woman. It would have been foolish of me to expect my friend to go door knocking with me. Furthermore, I had no right to think that, because we used to play this silly game, she was unqualified to now guard the leaders of our church and the people who attended worship services. By this time, as a singer, preacher and teacher, I also held several leadership positions in the church. Lisa could not justifiably judge me as unfit to be a minister, because of the havoc I used to cause as a child prankster. We were the same people, but we were also different in many ways. We grew up! We were grown women! Our current relationship required new boundaries. I had to see Lisa in a new light, and she had to do the same with me.

Oddly enough, the Meekins family was also life-long members of this church that Lisa and I later joined. This is a true story! (It only proves that this great big world we live in is really a small and very connected place!) I am grateful to God they did not hold my childhood antics against me! Did they remember who I was and what I did as a little girl? You bet!! Everybody knew John and Irene's kids! Was I a pain in the neck to Mr. Meekins and his family? Absolutely!! But they realized that I was not that little girl anymore. I was now an adult with a husband and a family of my own. I was a gifted singer and a diligent worker in the church. It would have been unfair for them to keep me boxed in, because I used to *knock on doors and run*. We too had to establish new boundaries for this reconnected relationship. As we did, I enjoyed a wonderful friendship with Mr. Meekins daughter, Sandra and her husband Tony. We sang in the choir together, got together on weekends and our children went to pre-school with one another. Establishing and regularly revising boundaries is very important to having a life that flows with power.

Sometimes, the people in our lives do not want us to grow. They fear that our growth will result in a loss for them. Family members and friends are also often afraid for new people to come into our lives. They argue that we should be leery of new friendships, because people cannot be trusted. But God is a god of growth and expansion. If our aim is to love people unconditionally, to wish nothing less than God's best for everyone, and to be our best selves in all relationships, we have nothing to fear. The reality is you have the right to say who comes in and out of your life. You should not relinquish that power to anyone else. The power of God in you can give you the wisdom for setting your own priorities and establishing healthy boundaries for your life and your relationships. Unfortunately, many people give this power over to other people far too quickly. But you must be confident in who you are. Do not be afraid to explore new horizons. Avoid the habit of people pleasing that often exists through codependent relationships. The list could go on and on; however, the truth remains that that priorities and boundaries are of major concern for many people. I have seen people remain stagnant for years, even decades, because they are unwilling to do what it takes to live life on their own terms. As long as your terms are pleasing to God, you have nothing to worry about. So long as you are concretely sure that your decisions are aligned with God's will and purpose for your life, you must believe that God will fill every void and make up any difference that becomes necessary. Parameters – or boundaries – might mean that few people are in your life during certain seasons. However, the people who "make the cut" will matter where it counts the most.

Putting People Out and Letting People In

Here are a few helpful steps to help make sure that your parameters are properly established and enforced. I call it the process of ***putting people out and letting people in.*** I hope that it helps you in your pursuit of a life that is truly filled with POWER!

Deciding Who Comes and Who Goes

There is a story recorded in Mathew 9, about the daughter of Jairus, a leader of the synagogue. His daughter, a young girl around 12 years old, is sick and about to die. Even though Jairus is not a believer in or follower of Jesus, he goes to Jesus to get help for his daughter. Jairus is willing to put tradition aside, if it means his daughter will live. And, when Jairus meets Jesus, he begins to worship and proclaim his faith that Jesus can remedy his dilemma. Jairus' most pressing, prevalent and present need is for Jesus to heal his daughter. Many people who knew Jairus' former beliefs might not understand him now coming to the controversial Jesus for help. But Jairus cannot let whether or not people understand his decision impact what he chooses to do. Now is the time for Jairus to decide who will come and who will go.

It does not matter what your background is or how long certain people have been wallpaper in your life. There comes a time when you must decide what path will best serve your goals and objectives. Jairus made that decision and Jesus immediately responds to his request. Jesus agrees to help and heads towards Jairus' house. The lesson to be learned from Jairus is this: *Everyone cannot go the distance with you!* Many times, people will carry more baggage than they are able to sustain. As I said earlier, people must grow with you as you move forward in life. When they fail to do so, they become extra weight and baggage. They want to hold you hostage to the way you used to think, the way you used to act, and the things you used to do. Eventually, their presence becomes a tool that the enemy uses to snuff out the light of God and to stifle the expansion of God. I always say that God can never be more God than God is already. Tomorrow, God will be God to the same degree that God was God yesterday, the day before and 10 years before then. However, your *capacity for God* grows as you grow spiritually and surrender your life completely to God's control and guidance. Note the words to this song –

Increase my capacity for you.
Increase my capacity for you.
God erupt inside of me.
Inhale. Exhale.
Freely breathe into me. (Author – Jonathan Nelson)

What powerful words! We must allow God to expand and grow in our lives so that we can complete the perfect work already begun within us. For this to happen, we must have the right people in the right places fulfilling the right purposes in our lives. We must discern who should be in our lives and what purpose they serve. And people must be willing to grow with us as we grow. **If they will not grow, then they might have to *go!*** Remember, purposes can change and shift in focus. So, for some people the process of *going* does not necessarily mean they leave our lives. Rather, it might mean that they *go to another place – and serve another purpose –* in our lives.

Sometimes the decision on whether or not a person comes or goes in your life is not based solely on what *you* do. Quite often, your decision is a reaction to the actions of the individual. For example, not everyone will be able to understand spiritual shifts in your life. However, their failure to understand does not excuse your responsibility to fulfill your assignment. You must also have the courage and discipline to establish boundaries that make your personal and spiritual advancement possible. For some reason, Jesus took Peter, James and John with Him to the mountain of transfiguration. Somehow, these three had the ability to see Jesus in a way that others would not or could not. They had the *capacity* to participate in Jesus' expansion – to see him move closer to fulfilling His earthly purpose. And even then the disciples wanted to build a tabernacle and stay there forever; it was that awesome an experience. Suppose Peter, James and John had resigned from the Disciples Board, just because Jesus refused to erect a tabernacle on that mountain? What if Jesus had succumbed to the pressure of pleasing his followers and agreed to stay there? The world would have missed out on what came next – the triumphant resurrection of our Lord Jesus and the powerful, life changing ministry that followed!! Allow nothing – not a person, place, situation, experience or circumstance – to make you miss out on God's ***next*** in your life.

Make Room for Progress

Let's return to the story of Jairus and his daughter. Take a look at the first thing Jesus says upon entering the house: *"**Make room,** for the girl is not dead, but sleeping." (Matthew 9:24)*. In other words, Jesus put the people out of the room that had come only for a funeral and not a healing service. If you are going to experience God's miraculous move in your life, you must make sure that there is ample room for God to have complete control. Take caution that your life is not too crowded with people, agendas and activities. Make a commitment to be on guard for all distractions. Sometimes, there are too many voices in your head, and you cannot hear what God is telling you to do. There are too many "quality check points" that a message must clear for authentication. When you receive a word from God, you do not want to have to ask this person or that person what he or she thinks about it. Others time there are too many external pulls on your spirit. Many people are in your life to *look at you* or to *take from you*. That is fine, so long as there are also enough people who are in positions to *give to you*. You must be able to identify the "lookers" and "takers" as people who essentially take up "room" in your life. Lookers are people who are on the same level as you, and join in to watch as your life unfolds. Takers are those people who receive what you have to give and who benefit from what you pour of out. You don't want to end up on only the giving end, lacking a sufficient number of people who can pour into your life and bring benefit to it as well. Follow the precedent Jesus establishes here and make room. He cleared the room. He made sure there was ample space for what was about to take place – *a miracle!*

Jesus is standing on the sidelines of our lives saying, **"Can you hear me now?"** You cannot obey what you do not hear. Many of us are not obeying God and receiving the blessings of God, because we cannot hear God clearly. We must be willing to move everything, everybody, every place, every situation, and every circumstance out of the way. Then, we will have capacity to experience God, hear God and **respond** to God in ways that will bring desired results in our lives.

Remove the Doubters and Spectators

I often wonder why people allow the negative comments of others to stop them from doing something. I am sure you can remember at least one time where somebody talked you out of a great idea you had. It is difficult to realize that people frequently see *our lives* through the eyes of *their lives*. They will set limitations and restrictions on us, based mostly on what they feel personally can or cannot be done. But you must never allow the doubts of others to make you doubt yourself. You may not be great at everything, but there is at least one thing – a gift, talent, skill, idea or ability – inside of you that is both powerful and mighty. It is the one gift that will *make room for you,* and bring you great success. This is the activity that, if you put your mind and will to it, no one can outshine you at doing it. And I do not mean shining spectacularly in the sense that you will become an overnight sensation and known all around the world. That's not necessarily everybody's destiny. I mean sensational in that you will bring to God's earth an activity, event, idea, thought, or result that comes from inside of you and only you. You are a unique, hand-crafted, divine creation. Make up your mind that no outside influence will stop you from manifesting the awesome power of God in your life.

Jairus did an awesome thing when he asked for help for his sick daughter. Jairus' faith and persistence are the reasons why his daughter was able to live and not die. I'd say that was pretty magnificent. At least, I'm sure the daughter thought so. But not everyone felt that way.

> *"When Jesus came into the ruler's house, and saw the flute players and the noisy crowd wailing, He said to them, "Make room, for the girl is not dead but sleeping." And they ridiculed Him." (Matthew 9:23 & 24)*

In the house we see *"the flute players"* and a *"noisy, wailing crowd."* Today, they would be called professional mourners. These people really know how to give you a "good funeral" – regardless of whether they actually know the person or not. But in that day, Jewish custom required that people be buried immediately. These gatherers would have been the family members or friends who had come to mourn Jairus' daughter. For them, it was a done deal. They were going along according to their custom, because she was a good as dead to them. There was nothing left to do except bury her. But not for Jairus! I am not sure if the people waiting at Jairus' house knew where he was going or not, when he went to find Jesus. It is not clear whether he told them that he was going to find this Jesus – a man he heard could raise the dead. But it does say that when Jesus got there he said, *"The girl is not dead but sleep."* And the people *laughed him to scorn,* meaning that they laughed bitterly at him, and they mocked him. They were not there for a miraculous resurrection from the dead; **they were there for a funeral!** They had taken time from their busy schedules to put somebody in the ground, and that is all they were interested in. So, there's Jairus, a father who wants desperately to save his daughter, surrounded by a room filled with doubters and spectators! Therefore when Jesus gets there and is ready to perform this miracle, the Bible says that he first had to clear the room. In other words, Jesus put the people out who were only there to reinforce the fact that the daughter was already dead and gone. For them it was time for a funeral, but for Christ it was time for some fun! And these people were bona fide joy killers, so they had to go.

The same is true for you and me. Perhaps some people have already pronounced a death sentence over your life and put nails in your coffin. To them, your past is too grim for a miracle, and they just cannot believe that your future can be magnificent. While you were down on yourself, crying, complaining, whining, broke all of the time and in a state of perpetual sinful living, everything was fine. But when you decided that it was time for you to rise from your "death-like" situations, the rooms of your life were suddenly too crowded. Many people, who fit perfectly in your life before, now stick out like sore thumbs. Over time, areas of compromise have begun to close in on what you know you are called to do and what you know you can become. As you move forward in life and change from season to season, parameters must be revisited and reevaluated. It may have been wholly acceptable to sit around and "cry over" things before. But in order to have continual and repeated resurrection moments in your life, you must cease your crying, evict the professional mourners and make room for the manifestation of God's power.

Perhaps Jairus knew how the people might respond. This might be the reasons why he did not tell them in the beginning where he was going. Maybe he knew that they would try and talk him out of it and put doubt in his faith-filled heart. You have to be careful to whom you tell your dreams. Most doubters and spectators mean no harm. They are merely evaluating and analyzing your life based upon the facts that are present in theirs. Or, they are expecting you to respond now the same way as you did in the past. And then there are those people who will tell you what you cannot do, only to turn around and do it themselves. Be careful what you share, because the most vulnerable of all entities is intellectual property. Thoughts and ideas, once spoken, become the property of the universe. First come, first served. But even then, you have nothing to fret over. God gets all the glory and what is meant to be associated with you and birthed from you will manifest exactly as God planned.

Nevertheless, you must take the influence and impact of doubters and spectators in your life very seriously. The Bible says that Jesus did not perform many miracles at Capernaum, because of the abundance of doubters. Those in your immediate circle matter a great deal. The people who are closest to you and allowed to speak into your life will heavily impact the amount and quality of focus you are able to give to your divine assignment. God's complete work cannot be done in your life when you are surrounded by negative thinking people. We often sit back and wonder why there is such an intense struggle and why we cannot get ahead. The answer is often right in front of our eyes. Some people have out lasted their welcome and outlived their purpose. **PUT THE DOUBTERS OUT!** Be careful, be vigilant and be bold. Be more committed to your destiny and your future than you are to any relationship or individual.

However, you must be careful not to remove people from your life just because they tell you the truth, particularly those things you may not want to hear. You do not want to have only "yes people" around you. Your immediate circles must also consist of people who think differently than you. One true sign of weakness is to be intimidated by someone who has an opinion that is different. When I say "put the people out" – I mean those who NEED TO GO! Make sure you "keep the keepers!" They will bless your life immensely.

Make Time for Privacy

After clearing the house, Jesus goes into the room where the young girl is laying. He takes her hand and says to her, *"Talitha Cumi!"* – meaning damsel arise, and immediately she got up! Even after Jesus had everybody to leave, he still goes into a place that is even more secluded, so that he and the young girl could have some privacy. Perhaps if the father or mother had been in the room, they might have misunderstood what was about to happen. Maybe they would have asked Jesus to explain his behavior. The young girl might have hesitated to obey Jesus' command, if there were others in the room. Whatever the reason, one thing is clear. Jesus felt that there was a need for privacy.

For every person reading this book, the need for privacy is very common. Some things that God wants to do are for your eyes only. It the same as when you have that special someone in your life, you enjoy being alone with them and spending quality time with them. As much as ladies love their girlfriends and enjoy hanging out and having fun, when it is time for being with that special someone everybody else has to take a back seat. You do not have time to chit chat on the phone. You opt to put your phone on silent or turn it off all together. You certainly do not want any surprise visits. Your friends just have to understand that, for the time being, you are **unavailable!** Privacy. Intimacy. Quality time. These occasions call for special arrangements to be made. The same rule applies to your relationship with God. There are seasons when God must have preeminence. When you recognize these times, you will reap the benefits of the "private sessions." The term private session reminds me of the fitness regiment infomercials I frequently see on TV. The instructor always reminds the viewing audience that *normally a private session costs MUCH MORE!* However, for a limited time, the facilitator's expertise and knowledge are being made available to this INTENDED AUDIENCE at a *lower price!* I love it! For the same is true in the Holy Spirit. We have been offered an inside track into the holy of holies. The King of Kings and the Lord of Lords is beckoning us to come closer, come higher, and to go deeper. There are some things that we simply cannot obtain from God in the midst of a crowd. If we are willing to pay the *lowly price* of a season of isolation, a period of intense struggle, or the reality of a relationship shifting or ending, then we can reap huge benefits. For it is then and perhaps only then, that we can position our lives to experience a new dimension of divine power! Private sessions with God lead to increased manifestations of PUBLIC POWER. And this power is not only reserved for a "high time" at a church service. That, my friend, is life as usual. It is church as we have become accustomed to know it. I'm talking about a different kind of power. I'm referring to **LifePOWER!** This power is available to us to influence and ignite magnificent results in every dimension of our lives, to the glory of God.

Also, you must remember that some of the things that are hidden within your heart, only you and the Spirit of God can deal with. All hurt and pain are not meant for everyone to see. Once you are free and on the mend, then those around you can benefit from what you have gone through. <u>But the healing process requires privacy and intimacy</u>. In order for you to be like the Jairis' daughter and truly rise up from dead situations, you must be willing to go into the tombs, where some pretty scary skeletons are lurking. However, adequate time must be allowed for the complete work. Be careful not to bring people into your recovery process too quickly. Just because you have been able to avoid a particular behavior for a few months, does not mean you are quite yet ready to be of assistance to others who might have the same struggle. Don't confuse the statement that *all things work together for the good* to mean that *all things are for all people.* This is not always the case. You do not have to tell everything about you to everyone you meet. Some things are meant to be kept private and only the residual power that the experience brought about in your should be visible to the public. Blabbing about everything you used to do and everything you are still struggling with does not bring God glory or do much to help people. Those kind of public statements are not about God's power, they are more about individual weaknesses. People can benefit from your experience without knowing all of the intricate details of what was your experience. How? The answer is that experience teaches you compassion and gives you discernment for future reference. But first make sure that you are completely healed and fully recovered.

Lastly, please always remember that as you continue your walk through spiritual and personal development, there will additional times when you must come away to a quiet time with God. It is during these times, that additional covers and layers are peeled away, so that more private work can be done. This is the only way to maintain where you are, while at the same time continue to grow.

So, be careful not to allow your life to become so crowded that you lose sight of your parameters. Everyone needs time alone with themselves and with God, no matter how perfect or pristine their lives may be. In these private places, there is total understanding and no need for explanations. There is unconditional love and complete safety, so you can be totally exposed and utterly vulnerable without fear of rejection or public shame. God often has to work on you in private, so that you can be released publically. You do not need a crowd of witnesses to validate you. You have nothing to prove. Eventually the world will see what God had in mind when your name was spoken in eternity. For now, just enjoy the private time. Make room in your life for privacy and intimacy with God.

As you do, remember these word that I came up with to help me.

"Letting go is easy. It's watching people leave that becomes hard."
So when you let go, walk away and don't look back.
Look up. There's strength up there somewhere!!

A Few Closing Words of Advice

I hope by now you understand the utter importance of regulating the traffic in and out of your life. You must know who you are, your self-value and self-worth. You have a right to set a standard for those who have access to you. There are in fact some people who just do not make the grade for a spot in your inner circle. *It does not mean they are not great and wonderful people, it only means that they are not for you.* Too many times, we feel so badly about ourselves that we are happy somebody – ANYBODY – is paying us any attention at all. But not all attention is good attention. Be selective. Be evaluative. Be diligently determined to monitor the parking lots, driveways, streets, roads, highways, freeways and interstates in your life. Somebody may be in the parking lot when the better place for them is the freeway. Somebody may be on the highway, when God's divine assignment for your life is in your driveway.

Be willing to move to new levels. Do not limit yourself to where you have always been. A new frontier is intimidating and challenging, but making the steps towards it is tremendously rewarding. I know it sounds harsh, but it is true nonetheless. **People are not expendable, but your relationships with people are**. It may be time for a person to be someone different to you. Don't be afraid to put the people out of an expired place. Do not be afraid to be alone. Make room for your relationship with God. Get rid of any and all excess baggage. Simplify your life. Prioritize your time. Put Jesus first, at all costs. Stop being a talker only and become a doer. Put all the doubters, mockers and spectators out. Give them freeway access only. Waive to them as you pass one another on the highways of life. Learn how to be intimate with God and how to cherish quality time alone as well. Be yourself when you are alone with God; the truth is already known anyway. If you feel a person is holding you back, put them out. Shucking and jiving? Not serious about God and righteous living? Trying to keep you in a box? Put them in their proper place, and re-touch the parameters of your life. Then, move on to pursue and receive God's supernatural power for your life.

12 Steps to Proper Parameters

As I have taught on this subject over the years, God has inspired me to develop several affirmations to help people gain the inner strength to establish proper parameters for their lives. By applying these truths, you can shift people to the right positions in your life. Here are twelve of my favorites.

****

1. *Recognize* that YOU are the REAL *guest of honor in your life.*
2. *Recognize* that for each new level, usually someone or something has to go.
3. *Recognize* WHO you are <u>and</u> WHERE you are.
4. *Recognize* **seasons** – *they are ALWAYS changing.*
5. *Recognize those who are good <u>for</u> you – not those who look good <u>to</u> you.*
6. *Recognize* the dead weight.
7. *Obey God **immediately.***
8. Be completely *honest* with others and ***yourself.***
9. Be especially *selective* about who shall remain.
10. Be content with solitude.
11. Be prepared for public scrutiny
12. Be committed to your destiny.

Principle #4 – Planning
<u>Planning is EVERYTHING!</u>

*Jeremiah 29:11 says, "For I know the thoughts that I
think toward you, says the Lord, thoughts of peace and
not of evil, to bring you to an expected end."*

****

You must have a plan for your life, and you must follow that plan with
unwavering diligence. Although not at all easy, the process is actually
quite simple. Even God uses the system of planning. And if God takes
the time to design a plan for our lives, we should be wise and plan as
well. The statement "if you fail to plan, you plan to fail" is so true. Most
of us heard this repeatedly as children. Our parents and elders were
trying to teach us the importance of goals, objectives, focus and strategic
planning. They understood that life is the finished portrait of the paint
strokes made by each choice we make. That's right – every choice you
make shows up on the picture that is your life! And if we can tune into
our divine assignments early in life and use them as the compass for
our path, then we will likely be guided to make better choices. And if
we make better choices then we can have better lives.

> *"A man's heart plans his way, but the Lord directs his steps."*
> *Proverbs 16:9*
>
> *"Plans are established by counsel; by wise counsel wage
> war." Proverbs 20:18*

The word plan means *a scheme or method of acting that is developed in advance; a specific project of definite purpose.* In other words, when you create a plan you must think it through ahead of time. You should not want until you are already mid-way through the experience to try and figure out how you will navigate through it. Figure out your strategy ahead of time. Also, a well thought out plan is <u>specific</u> and <u>targets a particular purpose</u>. Therefore, you might need more than one plan to cover all your dreams and aspirations. After you determine what your life's goals and vision are, you then have to break the big picture down into smaller components. Each component will most likely require its own plan. The plans will connect to and support one another. But if any part of the dream is not thoroughly planned out, the overall picture will be distorted and realization inevitably hindered.

Without a plan a person will wander aimlessly through life. Do you remember when grown-ups asked you, *"What do you want to be when you grow up?"* We would give answers such as a doctor or a lawyer or a teacher or a basketball player or a fireman. Whatever else would come to our minds at the time was a possible option. Then, these same grownups would advise us to be attentive in school, to work hard and get good grades. We were advised to stay out of trouble and to show respect to all elders and everyone in authority. They would impart other words of wisdom such as, *"Love can wait. Don't have any children yet. You've got your whole life to settle down. See the world!"* Do you remember those conversations?? I do! Do you wish you had listened more?? ***I certainly wish so***!

This advice essentially amounted to the individual parts of an effective plan that, if followed, would lead to success. The information was the foundation of the plan to keep moving forward. Eventually, you learn about life and meet other people who could help move your dreams forward to the next level. You come to understand that each level calls for the creation of a new plan or the modification of already established plans. As you make connections and come in contact with people who have similar interests, you refine your plan. Mentors, role models, advisors and sponsors will also play important parts in the planning process.

Successful people understand that planning is essential to success. And sticking with a plan is the key to accomplishing goals and not wasting years and years trying to find yourself or figure out who you are. The fact that you can see your reflection in the mirror every morning is proof that you are not lost! Make a decision today to live a life filled with purpose, instead of allowing life to **LIVE YOU**. Without a plan, life becomes a series of events that just happen, without meaning. What people call "living" is really an attempt to stay above water by rolling with the punches as they come. But God does not intend for you to live your life rolling with the punches. God intends for you to plan each punch strategically and have **an expected end in mind with each blow we throw.** Have you ever seen a person in a fight swinging sporadically and randomly, winding their arms up link a windmill? What usually happens? They tire out quickly! Or worse, they get hit right on the chin and down they go. The more skilled fighter just waits until the right moment to land a punch that knocks the opponent out. Again, having a clearly defined plan is better than winging it, **every time!**

You must realize that life is journey, and you will discover many things about life along the way. This discovery takes place whether you are guided by a plan as not. Life will happen whether you are prepared for it or not, so equip yourself to make the most of the journey. Let the journey teach you **and** take you somewhere at the same time. Unfortunately, many people find themselves very advanced in age with a lot of wisdom but very little success to show for it. Just one conversation with them leaves you speechless. You wonder how a person can know so much about so many different things and still remain stuck at Point A in terms of accomplishments and advancements. In many cases, all that is missing is **a plan**. This does not have to be the case. As a follower of God, you have a wonderful alternative insurance policy. You can trust that your times are in the hands of an all-knowing God. And even when you feel that your life is completely out of whack and the plan you have in place is most likely to fail, you can still have faith in God. God knows things that you do not know. God understand things that you cannot begin to fathom. The reason God knows more is because God drew up the plan for each of your life, even before you got here. So, even though you might not know the intricate details and workings of God's plan, rejoice at what you do know.

"Our soul waits for the LORD; He is our help and our shield. For our heart shall rejoice in Him, because we have trusted in His holy name." Psalm 33:20 & 21 (NKJV)

When you understand that God is in control and that God can be trusted to shield you, you can rejoice and wait patiently for the plan to unfold. You can also be assured that the plan will not just unfold, but it will bring about a great advantage. When God works things out, the end results always go in your favor. The only possible result is *added benefits* for those who believe in faith. Even if the process is uncomfortable, inconvenient, and unfamiliar, stick with the plan. You must know that going with the plan is much more advantageous to you. When you consider how God puts a plan together, there are even more reasons to rejoice. God's track record at success is all the more reason for you to forsake all other agendas and go with God's plan for your life. Your blessing comes as you follow through with whatever God is instructing you to do.

There will be questions, because when you start out you usually have no idea where God's plan will take you. Here again, to gain strength, go back to what you know for sure. What are the typical characteristics of God's plans? What are the guarantees? How can you stay with a plan that does not appear to be working out for your good? These are very meaningful questions. If they are settled once and for all, then you can concentrate all of your power and ability towards moving forward and gaining the results from life that you truly desire. I came up with three sure things that you can count on in God's plan.

Three Guarantees of A "God Plan"

God's Plan is Spectacular!

Expect nothing less than spectacular things for your life. A few synonyms for the word spectacular are *breathtaking, hair-raising, dramatic, impressive, striking, outstanding, prominent, and salient.* Wow! What a family of words. We have been conditioned to believe that we should expect the worst and hope for the best. However, the reality is that you usually get what you expect, even if you are hoping for better. Because your mind creates what you truly believe will happen you must be careful regarding your earnest expectations. For it is what you expect to happen that will show up in your life. I often say that our lives are a reflection of what we **truly believe.** Some people focus only on having hope, leaving their expectations to chance. This mentality leaves a back door open for doubt to enter your life. When you have real hope, you can believe (or expect) for anything because your **hope is in an Almighty God and the promises found in His Word.**

This is why when you understand that God is the author of your destiny you begin to realize that you should not only just hope for the best, you should *expect it!* Anticipate that your future will be breathtaking. Visualize that the blessings coming to you will literally make the hair on your arms stand up. Comprise a plan that is so awesome and powerful that an ordinary person would be terrified by it. Make sure that the plan for your life challenges your faith and makes a demand on your God. Never settle for mediocrity, because God had excellence in mind when He created you. Therefore, you must dare to dream big, magnanimous possibilities for your future. Take the challenge to respond honestly to questions like, *"If you could have your dream job tomorrow, what would it be?"* For many years, even until recently, I could not really answer this question. This is mainly because 1) I had never really considered what my dream job could be; 2) I had never imagined that I could really possess a dream job if I could think of one; and 3) I had mostly lived my life from the perspective of "making do" – not *"making dreams."* What a diminished, restricted approach to life this is.

As you dream for great things, remember that having the "spectacular" is not limited to simply to material things. You do not have to focus on getting stuff; most people who do find that more things really do not make you content or fulfilled. Furthermore, when you truly tap into what God has planned for your life, everything else will fall into place. Lining up with your divine destiny puts you on the path towards a life filled with the spectacular. God is faithful to purpose, destiny and divine plans! God's Word promises that the plan for your life is a plan filled with peace, love and joy in the Holy Spirit. In Jeremiah 29:11, you have the reassurance that God has plans to take care of you and to keep you from all evil, harm and danger. Prosperity, health and inner well-being are also parts of God's plan for you. You can rest assured that you will never be left alone or be without love. With these guarantees in place, you can reach for the stars, trusting that as you go in faith God will also provide for your every need.

Children of wealthy people rarely go to college just to get a job. They are there to pursue their passions, interests and dreams. They believe that if you do what makes you happy, money will come. Athletes who train for the Olympics are able to focus on training and practicing, so that they can be the very best in their particular event. They are not concerned about their living expenses, because they have family members, government programs and other sponsors who take care of those things for them. You might not be the child of a wealthy person and you probably do not have sponsors, but you do have the backing of the God of the Universe! You are "funded" by the one who *owns the cattle on a thousand hills!*

> Psalm 24:1 says, "The earth is the Lord's and the fullness thereof: The world, and they that dwell therein."

Move forward with your dreams in this confidence. God's got you covered! Live like you are the child of royalty – because you are! And when fear tries to grip your mind with reminders of obstacles and challenges, remember who is backing you. Your life does not have to be spectacular in comparison to anybody else's life. It only has to be *exceeding abundantly above all that* you *can ask or think.* The word tells us to try God – to prove God – which means to put God to the test of His Word. This biblical command puts us in the position to receive the spectacular things that God has lined up for each and everyone one of us.

Before I learned this principle, whenever I would think of a something great I wanted to do, I would immediately begin to evaluate what it would take to get it done. I considered the task from every angle, including the things that might keep me from being successful. For years, I thought this made me wise, prudent, analytical, and logical. I was a thinker and I was very good at it. But eventually, all I thought about were the problems. I began to focus only the negative. Then the dream became to be about the problems, instead of the about dream. Through prayer and self-reflection, I discovered that I was thinking my way right out of my dreams. I was rationalizing my way out of the spectacular future that God had ordained for my life. This is why I am admonishing you to guard your heart against an overly negative analytical process. Yes, you must use wisdom and there is such a thing as seasonal timing. But neither of these means that you cannot plan to do things that literally blow your natural mind. It only means that the bigger your dream, the harder you must plan. The Bible says that there is an answer for everything under the sun. It also tells us that *the Holy Spirit searches all things, even the deep things of God.* Furthermore, *the answers are **revealed to us by the Holy Spirit.*** Therefore, God can reveal to you tactics and strategies to overcome every negative image of impossibility that pops up in your mind. We will talk more about this in the next section.

As long as God is at the center of your plan, there are no limits. God can do anything and so can you. *You can do all things through Jesus Christ who gives you strength.* Either the Word of God is true or it's not. And, it is either all true or none of it is true. And I believe the Word to be both TRUE and THE TRUTH. God's Word is totally, absolutely and completely trustworthy. So, when you are thinking about the plan for your life, go for the spectacular.

God's Plan is Specific

I mentioned in the previous section how God can give you strategies and tactics to overcome any obstacle you face. You need this information to make sure that you are moving forward at the right time, to the right place, to do the right thing. You must make sure that you are following God's plan for you and not God's plan for somebody else. Be sure to avoid running after what everybody else is doing or going where everybody else is going. God's plan for you is specific, and it is tailor-made just for you.

This is where many people miss the miracle of following a plan given by God. God does not just stop with the big picture. On the contrary, God is also into details. Everything about God's creation – all of what you see around you – is comprised of details. There are natural systems and processes in place that govern the earth, to keep things in order and running smoothly. All of this requires details and specifics. Remember, we are supposed to follow God's example. God has a set time to bless us. God is a god of seasons, and nothing in God is ever premature or late. God' timing is perfect.

Psalm 102:13, "For you shall arise and have mercy on Zion. For the time, yeah the set time to favor her has come."

God is very specific about what is in store for you. Each hair on your head is numbered. Every aspect of your DNA is peculiar to only you. No one else has your same finger print or genetic structure. Every detail of your existence, down to the exact minute of your life experiences, is set in place before you were even conceived. When it comes to the decisions you make in life, adopt this same philosophy. Seek God first, follow the teachings of Jesus Christ and live a life that is pleasing to God according to His Word. Then, your plans will automatically line up with the plan of God. I believe this is what the Bible means when it says, *"If we delight ourselves in the Lord, then he will give us the desires of our hearts."* When your heart is in the right place, you will want what God wants. You will pursue what you believe God is leading you to do. It might be totally different from what anybody else is thinking or doing. But that is alright, because God is going to give you the grace and the strength – and the specific details – to be successful.

Nevertheless, you still need an outline that guides you through each step of the plan. Break your spectacular dream down into stages, phases, and lessons to be learned. And then, *write the vision* for each one, *and make it plain* how you will navigate through the journey. You must also become a student of your craft, in order to master it as much as possible. Learn all that you can; become knowledgeable about what you are planning to do. Having faith is not an excuse to be ignorant or vague. In fact, faith is what moves you into action and pushes you into areas where you might not have imagined you could go. A belief that God has your back allows you the freedom to ask questions, conduct research, partner with others and develop a specific plan to realize your dream. Wise people know that a plan for the spectacular is really *a series of plans* outlining the details of where you want to go, how you plan to get there, and what resources you need to be successful. Effective plans include benchmarks – or established intervals – where you can evaluate your progress. When planning for your life, set short-term and long-term goals for yourself, and then put your confidence in God to order your steps and bring things to pass. And remember that your plan is your plan. It is the sketch for your life. Do not compare yourself to other people. Never judge your level of success by someone else's accomplishments. Know your place, and stay in your lane. Play your position and play it well. Be only who you were created to be. And call the things into your life that are necessary and relevant to what you want to accomplish. Use your faith and biblical principles to navigate through every stage and season, on your way to destiny and purpose.

God's Plan is Solid

One of my favorite hymns is *"My Hope is Built."* I especially love the chorus which says *"On Christ the solid rock I stand. All other ground is sinking sand! All other ground is sinking sand."* These words remind us of how firm God's plan is for our lives.

You can trust God to do exactly what God promised. As Paul promised the passengers of that doomed ship, *"It will be exactly as God said." (Acts 27:25)* The same assurance belongs to you. What God has planned is automatically secure, firm and settled. You can be confident that God will fulfill His promise to you. God will be faithful to the Word he declared over your life. God's plan is indeed **SOLID**. The word "solid" means of substantial character; not superficial; without openings or breaks; firm, compact in substance; without separation or division; continuous.

> *Hebrews 10:22 -23 tell us, "Let us draw near with a true heart in full assurance of faith . . . Let us hold fast the profession of our faith without wavering (for He is faithful who promised)"*

The reason why you can rest assured of the validity and reliability of God's plan is because God is faithful to his Word. The *will* of God is revealed in the *Word* of God. The Word of God teaches you how to think like God, so that you can live your life in faith and not fear. In order to fully embrace the confidence of what God is going to do you must know what God says in His Word. The Word of God also reveals what God has in store for each and everyone who loves Him and who seeks to live lives of service that are pleasing to Him.

When I was growing up, we used to have a slang word to indicate when something was right on the money, absolutely positively true. When we really meant something, we would say "Solid!" Today, they use words and phrases like *"my dog"* and the *"N-word"*. But we would say, "Solid!" That meant it was settled! Done! There was no doubt about it. You could take what we were saying directly to the bank. If our friends told us to meet them at our favorite restaurant, and we were definitely going to there – *Solid!* If we told someone that we would pick them up and give them a ride somewhere – *Solid!* This is exactly how you should view God's promise to you regarding the spectacular and specific plan that He has for your life.

> *Matthew 7:11, "If you then, being evil, know how to give good gifts to your children, how much more shall your Father in Heaven give good things to those who ask Him?"*

Just like you have faith and trust in a loyal friend, you can have faith and trust in the promise and the plan of God. God wants you to know that you can go to sleep at night, because He never does. God wants you to dry your eyes and hold your head up high no matter what, because His plan is solid. God is going to come through for you. Everything that you are standing and believing for in faith is as good as done. All you have to do is to stand on the God's Word, be faithful, obedient and diligent in God's plan. Follow the specific instructions you are given, and your blessing will manifest in due season.

> *Jeremiah 29:12 says, "You will call upon me and go and pray to Me, and I will listen to you."*

That's a solid! That is a guarantee that we can take to the bank!

> *Verse 13 goes on to say, "You will seek me and find me, when you search for me with all your heart."*

Another Solid! And verse 14 wraps up this particular promise,

> *"I will be found by you and bring you back from your captivity."*

Again, a great plan is a solid plan. S-O-L-I-D! When you establish your plan on divine principles and truths, you are guaranteed to have success. And the great news is *there are so many wonderful biblical promises and universal truths that you can stand solidly on!* So, what is your new response to the enemy? You got it. **SOLID!** When doubt and fear try to intimidate you from moving forward with your plan, just yell SOLID!

SOLID – You're coming out on top!
SOLID – You've got the victory!
SOLID – You are delivered!
SOLID – Your marriage is restored!
SOLID – Your body is healed!
SOLID – Your life is blessed!
SOLID – Your best days are ahead of you!
SOLID – With God, all things are possible!

Principle #5 -- Performing
<u>Just Do It</u>

You've heard this phrase many times before, from the famous shoe brand, Nike. Unfortunately, life is not always that simple, or we would have "*just done it*" a long time ago. Janet Jackson's song, *What Have You Done for Me Lately,* reminds us that life is about more than just what you say. Life is also about what you do. You must be a productive person, in one way or another, in order to experience a fulfilling life. So, on your quest to discover a life filled with power and results, you must understand how you can go from dreaming about doing great things, to actually accomplishing great things. Another phrase we hear all of the time comes straight from the Bible.

> "*I can do all things through Christ which strengthens me.*"
> *(Philippians 4:13)*

I told you earlier in this book that I was going to challenge your thinking a bit with a simple, two-word question. Here it is again, *"So what?!?"* You say that you can do all things through Christ, because through your relationship with Jesus Christ the power of God is alive on the inside of you. **BIG DEAL!!** Simply having the power available to you does not mean that you know how to actually tap into the power and maximize it. To do this, requires that you ask yourself some very hard questions. For example, what are *you* going to do, so that you can move from simply being **strengthened** to do all things, to **actually doing all things?** How are you going to make sure that your life is better, because of your faith in this particular scripture? What have the practices of positive affirmation and scripture quotes actually produced in your life? Remember, Diligent Delores? Do you recall how she went to conference after conference and followed preacher after preacher? Nevertheless, her life was not any better. That is because she was a *hearer* only and not a *doer*.

Your faith must provoke you to action. Otherwise, you will not experience a highest possible degree of supernatural power in your life. Again, I am not talking about just naming and claiming things. There are other ways to be blessed, besides money, cars, houses and other materialistic blessings. For some people, they need power to have peace and maintain joy when facing monumental life challenges. Regardless of what your situation may be, carrying your Bible and quoting your favorite scripture will produce minimal results unless you are prompted to follow through with what must actually be done. Only people who have the diligence and discipline to apply biblical and spiritual principles to a plan can be called **performers,** who are able to actually see results.

Life is Doable!

I know that you may feel overwhelmed with way too many things to do. Welcome to the Club of Life! Nevertheless, you must understand that no matter what you are faced with – *it's all doable.* You will need a plan and you must stick to your plan, but success is absolutely possible. Not only is success possible, it is promised to those who will use the keys to success and principles of personal discipline to bring about the desired results.

> *Joshua 1:8 says, "This Book of the Law shall not depart from your mouth, but you shall meditate in it day and night, that you may observe to do according to all that is written in it. For then you will make your way prosperous, and then you will have good success."*

Through patience, endurance and diligence you can master the art of what I call *doing life!* You will understand how to get from Point A to Point B, and how to have Point B look exactly as you had imagined. It won't necessarily be easy, and you may need to regroup every now and then. The principles discussed in this book must also become a road map to you. But if you are determined to perform at your highest level possible, there is nothing that anyone can do to stop you from doing so. If there's a goal you desire to obtain, map out the steps it will take to get there. Add of the cost for each step and develop a strategy for moving forward. Be prepared for challenges, obstacles, detours and setbacks. Success also requires that we stay focused and make sacrifices when making life choices. For example, if you have dreams of owning your own business, then you must be careful with how you manage your personal finances. If your goal is to get out of debt, you will need a budget that you strictly follow, and frivolous purchases and excursions will have to wait. Dave Ramsey said it very well, "If you can live like nobody else, then you can live like nobody else." In other words, if you can suffer through conditions that few others are willing to endure, then you can enjoy a life that few others are able to enjoy. As you work towards your goals, you will undoubtedly feel as if what you are aiming for will never happen. But it will! Do not lose hope. Right inside of you is the God-kind of ability to get it done. Have faith in yourself and have faith in God! And then, allow your faith to inspire you with a *list of things to do*. Move forward knowing that with God all things are possible if you will only believe.

Hebrews 10:23 says, "Let us hold fast the profession of our faith without wavering, for He is faithful who promised."

The process is the same whether or not you need to fortitude to finish your college degree or to refrain from an ungodly act. You must do the work! My husband, Pastor Marvin E. McCoy, often says, *"God is not going to do for you, what you can do for yourself!"* Those words are so powerful. Too many times, people want things to happen overnight, just because somebody prays and agrees with them. Prayer and agreement controls what happens in the spirit realm. When two people touch and agree in faith, absolutely nothing is impossible. However, your fortitude and diligence will determine what happens in the physical realm. They dictate what you will actually see manifested in your life. Our job is to figure out what we must do in order to get what is already done and settled in the spirit realm to be realized in our physical lives. Countless believers will never truly be free and delivered, because they do not want not do the work that is so necessary. They do not want to endure seasons of isolation or preparation. They give up too soon from trying to reprogram their mind and thinking through prayer, mediation and study of God's word. No trip to the altar, no amount of oil, no encounter with the carpet will do these things for you. Only you can. And, believe me when I say, **YES YOU CAN!**

Perform No Matter What ~ No Excuses Allowed!

Do you feel that you have wasted too much time and missed too many opportunities? So, what! You can still perform anyway! Performers are not exempt from challenges. Performers merely learn how to overcome them. These two challenges – wasted time and missed opportunities – are still no reason to give up and forsake your dreams. Perhaps you can identify with the heartbreak that these two can bring. You know what it feels like to play catch up with bodies that are older, minds that are slower, and energy that is weaker. Looking back at what might have been can hinder your progress in reaching your goals. You might wish you had finished college earlier, started your career sooner, or given more quality time and love to your children. Perhaps you wish you had begun a life of faith while you were younger. You ponder as to why you did not save more money, eat less food and give that guy with potential your phone number **before** he hooked up with the girl next door! Wasted time and missed opportunities can either hinder you or help you. It is easy to get discouraged and feel that your time has passed and you missed your boat. And maybe you did. But again I ask that thought-provoking question – **so what??** If you missed one boat, another one has got to be on its way because God will never let you drown in the waters of life. Go back to the drawing board. Return to the basics! Get to doggie paddling. Stop whining, complaining and living your life in *Woulda-Coulda-Shouldaville, USA.* Do what you've got to do, until the next boat sails through. And if the next boat is taking too long, BUILD YOUR OWN BOAT! Whatever you do, do not give up. While you are out there in the middle of the ocean called your life, feeling as if you will drown at any moment, you are learning valuable lessons that will benefit people you have yet to meet. You can help the next person be ready the first time around! You will be able to share your knowledge and allow others to learn from your experiences.

You've heard it before, *"Aint nothing to it but to do it!"* And yes you can do it, because there is divine, supernatural energy and power inside of you, strengthening you to manifest the life you desire. You possess the same power that enabled Christ to totally satisfy his earthly mission, even though doing so caused him rejection, persecution, controversy, conviction, and execution. To his accusers, doubters and abusers, *Jesus said not a word.* You know why? Because Jesus was empowered by God to succeed no matter what. He was not strengthened to whine about the pain, struggle and cost of getting the job done. My friend, neither are you. If you apply the principles that Jesus lived by to your life, you can overcome as well. You will survive unimaginable circumstances to render the performance of a lifetime. Do not cry over spilled milk. Do not waste your strength and energy blaming the world and everybody in it for your past failures and mistakes. Accept that these things happen in everyone's life. Make up your mind to get over them and to get on with your life, so that life does not get over on you! Yes you can do *ALL THINGS!* What things? The things you dream about doing. Wake up from apathy and do what it takes to realize your dreams. Implement that plan. Move forward with that idea. Take the risk and believe that God will back you up with everything you need. You have all that we need to triumph and to be successful.

Now, while you're out there doggy paddling, there are a few things you must remember to do at all times. If you do, performing at a high level will become a way of life for you. You can transition from merely dreaming about great and mighty things, to actually doing them with your life. Here are a few more helpful hints to help you along your journey.

Stay Focused

> Isaiah 26:3 says, *"Thou wilt keep him in perfect peace whose mind (thoughts and imagination) is stayed on thee; because he trusted in thee."*

You must understand that what you believe determines your how you think. And, how you think determines what manifests in your life. As the saying goes, *it's a mind thing.* You must focus your mind over whatever may be "the matter". If you believe something in your heart long enough and rehearse it in your mind, it will manifest in your life. Be it positive or negative, it will show up. For example, a perfect work has already been started inside of you. You must now internalize the truth that as you journey throughout life, the vision will unfold. If you earnestly believe that the greatness already inside of you has an appointed time to be revealed, you can stay focused on the things you must do in order to participate in that process. Focusing your mind on the right thing is the key. Focus on what you have planned to achieve, and no one will be able to keep you from doing it. Realize that you become what you practice. Unfortunately many people practice all the wrong things. Defeat, depression, regret, failure, anger, unforgiveness, and all of their distant cousins keep showing up in their daily lives. They have reoccurring roles in the dramas that play their in our minds and manifest in their relationships. For some reason, people act surprised when they see these things spring up and have to deal with them. They are surprised despite the fact that these negative realities are exactly what they rehearse repeatedly. People are experts at negative thinking. Focusing on and thinking about the positive feels foreign, and many are ill-equipped to undo the old patterns and replace them with new ones. As a result they cannot move forward to develop and implement plans to actuate the divine power available to them to turn their circumstances around in our favor. Ask yourself the important question, *"How is what I'm doing working for me?"* If your answer is that your life is not working the way you want it to then practice focusing on a new one. Your new assignment is to practice being whole, complete, fulfilled and satisfied in the minds of our spirit. Rehearse living a fulfilling life of passion, purpose, destiny and dreams that is based on God's word and a divine plan that you are totally committed to walking out. Where is all of this practicing and focusing going to take place? I'm glad you asked. Keep reading.

For the next few hours, take note of every time your thoughts of yourself or your situation are negative. Don't try to alter your thoughts at first. Simply note if there is a negative pattern. Record the negative thought this way: *I am feeling negative about* _____, *because I believe* _____. The key here is to capture the underlying <u>belief</u> that you are holding as <u>truth</u>.

You may also use the work "fear" instead of the word "believe". Here is an example.

> ***I am feeling negative about my child's poor behavior in school, because I believe people will think I have not done a good job in teaching him/her right from wrong***

This is a power practice that is not always easy. Many times you are told to simply pretend as if the negative thought is not there. Other times you are admonished to simply put it out of our minds. But this exercise helps you to acknowledge the reality of what you are calling "truth", based on what you earnestly believe (or focus on repeatedly). Faith is a divine principle that works, regardless of the objective. Your life is a reflection of what you truly BELIEVE. If you do not like what you see, then change what you believe. To do this, you must shift your focus to a divine truth that can change your beliefs. Replace every faulty, defeated belief with powerful, positive promises. Remember, unless you change what you truly believe, your life will never change. You can say, "I am the head and not the tail" all day long. But unless you truly grow spiritually and personally to believe it, you will only see change to a minimal degree. As you become more aware of the negative thought patterns and do the self-work of challenging them with a positive, divine truth, eventually the way you thing will change. You can stay focused by setting goals, establishing priorities, and being selective.

1. *Setting Goals*

Another practice that will help you to stay focused is to set goals. Goals help to direct your efforts and energies, while reducing the likelihood that distractions will deter you. Furthermore, you must be careful to set *realistic goals*. It is senseless to overburden yourself trying to do everything you are dreaming about in the span of one year. Also, avoid wearing yourself down and overextending yourself, simply because half the year is gone and you have yet to realize your accomplishments. Whatever you are worrying about over can wait another day. You might feel as if time is running out, but that is impossible. Time cannot be owned or manipulated by the events that take place in life; time is beyond human control. Time belongs to God, and God has perfect time management skills. You might not believe this, but you are right on schedule, even if you feel you have wasted years. Because your path is just that: *your path.* The great potential inside of you will be maximized. You can fulfill all that is within your heart, before the end of *your time,* if you commit to staying focused. Stay focused on the principles you have read in this book – *your potential, purpose, plan, and parameters* – and you will soon see that you really possess the power to do things you'd never imagined possible.

> *Numbers 23:19, says, "God is not a man that he should lie nor the son of man that he should repent. Has he said, and will he not do it? Or has he spoken, and will he not fulfill it?"*

This verse confirms that God will not have to apologize at the end of your life for unbroken promises. Whatever has been declared over your life can come to pass and be fulfilled, if you can manage to just stay focused. Watch out for distractions and do not allow yourself to become sidetracked. Use your goals and milestones as the barometers that gauge your life. Make *everything and everybody* coincide with your goals and your dreams. That's focus! Every decision – how much money you borrow, the friends you choose, the relationships you sustain, the time for starting a family – *even if you are married,* the types of purchases you make, how much house or car you buy, how much education you acquire – must all support your desired outcome. If you move off course and "give yourself some *me* time", then you will enjoy the immediate pleasures of your reprieve, but your future might pay the consequence. Being focused on goals sometimes means that you postpone a few pleasures. But I believe that what you get in the long run is better than what you may (or may not) enjoy in the right now. Being broke is never fun. However, it is a much more enjoyable situation when you are a broke *college student,* as opposed to a *broke adult with adult financial obligations and commitments obligations!* For example, dropping out of college to get a job and make money, sounds like a great idea when you are 19 and 20 years old. At that age, $20,000 seems like a fortune! But think about how your earning power might be affected in 10 years, when you are 30 years old. Consider if you will be able to realize your dream without an education. I've discovered that sometimes having money leads you to make decisions where you need to make more and more money. Say you have a job. You need clothes for that job, but you do not really make enough money to buy the clothes you want. So you get a credit card to buy them. Now you are not working to make and save money, you are working to pay your credit card bill. Or, you might need a car to get to back and forth to your job. So, you go out and buy a car, because you have to get to work. Now you are working to pay your credit card bill <u>and</u> your car note. Your focus is on other things, and your life will shift accordingly.

2. *Establish Priorities*

Focus is about priorities. If you lose focus on one priority prematurely to move on to something that seems more attractive at the time, you might miss out on a once in a lifetime opportunity. Take for example the matter of relationships, particularly in light of how they impact the priority of getting an education. If you're a college student focusing on your *relationship*, rather than your *studies*, you will likely move in the direction of the relationship. Taking the next step will seem natural and feel right to you. And, it may be; but then again it may not. Marriage is wonderful, and I earnestly believe that any two committed people can make a marriage work. However, not all relationships are intended to end up in marriage. The lack of focus can have you on the right path but at the wrong time.

The college experience is about more than just lectures and study halls. It's about seeing the world, meeting people, learning about other cultures. You develop as a person in many areas, such as mentally, spiritually, intellectually and emotionally. You make life-long friends and establish lasting connections. To truly enjoy this time of life requires that the majority of your time, energy and effort be focused on living in those moments. Priorities can help you realize just how large the world is, and how much of it is available to you. To be the best, priorities are mandatory.

3. *Be Selective*

I mentioned earlier in this book about how we are too lackadaisical in the standards of who comes into our lives. This is also true of the people who get to stay. Here is where the process of being selective becomes important. The Bible calls this *laying aside weights.* In order to maintain your focus, you must be careful to remove any and every weight that has attached itself to you. Sometimes this means letting people go who may have been in your life for many years. However, I've come to realize that people can become like cobwebs. They are just there hanging out in a corner, not causing any real trouble, until you run into them. Then they are all over the place and it becomes quite unnerving and disturbing. But until you disturb the place that they have occupied, or until you try to get them to move to *another place or level,* they are like wall candy. Just sitting there, not bothering anybody. For example, when you begin to broaden your horizons and expand your borders, new people will undoubtedly come into your life. The friends who are already a part of your life will often – all of a sudden – have boundary issues. Of if you begin to move in a direction that brings you closer to your purpose and your destiny – total obedience to the divine plan for your life – you may find that those who occupied the "background" of your life will unexpectedly want a front row seat. But do not be shaken or moved. Stay the course. Stay focused. Set goals. Establish priorities. Be selective. And fulfill your destiny. If you have made up your mind to go back to school, then go. If you have committed to joining a Bible class or attending church more regularly, be your own cheerleader and make it happen. If Wednesday mornings at 5 am is your newly appointed time for prayer and meditation – followed by 30 minutes of exercise – then without fail or excuse, be on your knees and in your Word on Wednesday mornings. If you want to get it done, you can get it done. But it is not going to happen by some mystical osmosis. You have to apply the principles! You must know who you are and what God has placed inside of you. Know what has been promised to you, and believe that these things are true. Have faith in God and faith in yourself. Do what *Hebrews 10:23 tells says and,* "*Hold fast to our confessions without wavering, for He is **faithful who has promised.**"*

Stay on Your Feet

I talked earlier about overcoming challenges and obstacles to reach your goals. One way to overcome and move forward is to learn how to stay on your feet. This means that you learn how to remain standing and to keep moving, no matter what the opposition. When you truly believe in your potential you develop the strength to stand on your own feet, regardless of what comes your way. You also gain the confidence that **your feet** are strong enough to keep you standing! Sometimes, the minute trouble comes into our lives we often begin to look for someone to help us. We look to our friends, family, prayer partners, and colleagues to support us, cheer us on, validate us, affirm us, and remind us that we are worthy. But the truth is that even when those people are available, hearing these things form them is never enough. If you do not believe that you can make it and that you are worthy, it doesn't matter who else does. They can scream it from the mountain top and write it across the sky with the Goodyear Blimp. But if what they are saying does not register with something that you already know about yourself, your response will likely be, *"You're just saying that!"* And you would be right, because if you do not believe it then the words of other people are just empty words.

Lack of confidence and resolve often come from constantly feeling as if you have a big red "X" on your chest. Perhaps you feel bombarded with one thing after another, and wonder if you are a target for trouble or, what I call, *a trouble magnet*. And you may be justified in feeling this way. But the reality is there is very little you can do about many of the unfortunate circumstances that come your way. Life is a hard struggle sometimes, with winding roads and curvy turns. If you are not careful, you fall into a victim mindset and feel that life is against you. But the truth is life could never be against you, because God is in control and God is on your side. You have been given inner strength and power (yes, LifePOWER!), to realize your potential, pursue your purpose, prioritize your plans, and establish your parameters. The presence of trouble does not change any of these promises to you. To take it a step further, adversity is not an excuse not to perform; it is not a reason to fall down off your feet.

Crying about your negative experiences will do you no good and get you nowhere fast. In fact, this behavior will only produce more of the frustrating, cyclical pattern of getting up and falling down over and over again. Take ownership of your thoughts and recognize your patterns. Know your triggers and develop strategies to diffuse them. Be watchful of things that easily upset or distract you. Be the captain of your own emotional ship. Find a way to stay on your feet and maintain forward progress, until more strength comes. Even if you cannot move forward at a particular moment, remain standing. Refuse to go give up and go backwards! Here are a few thoughts that can help you stay on your feet.

1. ***The Flood is On Your Side***

    Psalm 1:3 says, "I am like a tree planted by the rivers of waters. I shall not be moved."

This verse could easily read, *I shall not <u>easily</u> be moved,* meaning, that there will be opposition but it will not be able to simply knock you down. The potential and power inside of you empowers and enables you to stand through any storm and through any attack, because you have the power of God on your side. When life comes against you, stand in faith and believe that there is more going *for you* than that which is coming against you. There is another verse of scripture that says, *"When the enemy came upon me like a flood, the Spirit of the Lord lifted up a standard against them."* Usually "the flood" – or the power to destroy – is assumed to be on the side of your enemies. But you would just must move the comma up a little and put it in the right place. Put the flood on your side! *When the enemy came upon me,* **like a flood the Spirit of the Lord lifted up a standard against them!** With God on your side, you can stay on your feet. You might be staggering, but stay on your feet. There will be times when you are literally standing all by yourself. But I firmly believe that standing still while you wait is better than getting up after you fall. Whatever you do, stay on your feet!

2. ***Get the 4:11***

    Psalm 41:11 says, "By this I know that thou lovest me that you did not allow my enemies to triumph over me." I like to say that this scripture gives us **the 411 on *THE ONE!*** Fill your mind with the right information that will keep you from falling. Remind yourself continuously that God is bigger, greater, mightier, smarter, smoother, and sweeter than any negative situation in your life. And because God is superior, you are as well. Remember, the same power that exists in God abides in you. So stop worrying about your troubles or your enemies. You are still winning. You win every day that you get up and show up. You are still here! You still have hope! You still desire your best life! You are still employed! You are still married! You are still praising and rejoicing! You are still doing your life's work! You are still raising your children! Whatever your "still" may be *you are still here! You are still on your feet!* And that is a sign that there is yet more for you to do.

Stay Free

Sometimes it is difficult to mix what you *know* about yourself, with what you *believe* about yourself. You can experience wonderful revelations about the great person that you were created to be; however, when you are faced with the realities of everyday life, you can sometimes slip back into the same mindsets that keep you living the same kind of life. In order to be truly liberated and released for passion, power and purpose, you must do the work to stay free. You must diligently engage the principles that will allow you to keep the freedom you have been given and to talk in that liberty every day. One scripture verse puts it this way, *"Stand fast therefore in the liberty by which Christ has made us free, and do not be entangled again with a yoke of bondage." (Galatians 5:1)*

To be free means to enjoy personal rights or liberty, as a person who is not in slavery. I believe that it is every human being's right to have the opportunity to live out his or her passions and to realize full potential, in order to have optimal impact in the world. I often say, "When you live your life this way, you never really die, because the essence of who you are lives on in the lives of the people you touch." However, this mentality and life philosophy require freedom of the mind. You must be free from your past, free from tradition, free from your circumstances, and most of all free from other people's opinions, expectations and aspirations. And the most significant truth about being free is that *your freedom is YOUR JOB!* Nothing can grip you or have a hold on you, unless you allow it. No one can make you feel insignificant, rejected, inferior or insufficient unless you already believe that you are those things. Staying free begins with accepting responsibility for the fact that if you are feeling, thinking or living a particular way it is exactly that. YOU are the one feeling, thinking and living as you are. A wise mother once said, "Wherever you go, there you are!" In other words, being able to perform at your highest level is possible only if you determine that it is and that you are the one who must activate the power already given to you.

I know that many people look at being free in terms of a certain sin, behavior pattern or lifestyle that must be abandoned and abstained from. The freedom process then pertains to restraining your desires and refraining from these practices. This philosophy is true to some extent, and has no doubt helped countless people improve the quality of their lives. However, I believe that it is also limited. If this mindset is the extent of your freedom guarantee, then you might not be free for long. The sin is not limited to the act itself. Although space will not allow me to deal completely with the topic, allow me to briefly discuss the issue of sin. Sin by definition is that which is in opposition to God's benevolent purposes for his creation; an ever-present reality that enslaves humans individually and society collectively. Summarily, sin is that which seeks to separate you from God. Separation is not just a behavior it is also a position. Therefore, any undesirable behavior that a person portrays is a symptom of a condition. The behavior itself is not the condition. Take for example, swearing (or cursing). The sin is not so much the *words themselves,* but the spiritual unrest, anxiety or distress that is believed to have the power to so negatively impact a life, that the individual is driven to swear. The sin is in the belief that swearing is the best option. In that position of unbelief, doubt, worry, fear, anxiety – or whatever *dis*-ease you may be encountering, you have allowed yourself to become separated from God. So the truth is then, that a state of sin exists, ***whether you swear or not!*** So, if you want to be free from swearing, do not just try to change your speech. Change your thinking about your reality. Rest in the peace of God, and stand on what you know is really true. Do this, and eventually swearing won't be necessary.

A Final Word on Staying Free

Staying free is easier said than done. A relationship with God frees you from the slavery of circumstances, situations, traditions, generational limitations, and life itself. You are also free from the mindset that says *you can't or you won't.* In scripture, one way that freedom is portrayed is when an individual is released from a yoke. A yoke is something that is usually tied around the neck of farm animals to keep them moving in the right direction. The device was attached to their necks, to keep them from looking to either side and in doing so, it restricted their movement. From a spiritual perspective, a yoke not only restricts your movement, but it will also keep you tied to something or someone from which you desire to be free. For some people, the focus is to stay free from worldly things things, but they allow churchy things to bind them just as much. Religious traditions can be as restrictive as the old, destructive behaviors from your past. They tend to become consumed with people's opinions and expectations. What other people think becomes more important than what they are being told about themselves. Or worse, they begin compare themselves to people who are just like them. You would be surprised to discover that many people appear to be confident and secure, but they are just as afraid as the next person. But if you are not secure in your freedom, you will focus on outdoing the next person rather than performing at your highest level. And, that is not freedom at all.

The power of God That comes into your life, releases you from all restrictions – whether they be people, places, predictions or predicaments – that no longer serve who you really are. In this way, freedom with all of its benefits can come at a costly price. A *free place* might be confused with *a lonely place* by someone who is not mentally, spiritually and emotionally mature enough to handle it. The tendency might be to just go back to what is familiar. Hence the saying, "Better the devils you know than the angels you don't." What a foolish way of thinking! But as crazy as it may sound, many people live their lives this way. They encounter God in ways that others can only dream of. But when it is time to do what is necessary to stay free, they buckle at the knees, only to be entangled, tied up and MESSED UP all over again. Continuously repeating this process reinforces the fallacious thinking that true freedom – authentic peace, joy and happiness – is allusively unobtainable. But nothing could be further from the truth. You can handle being free! I decree it now. It might be hard and it might get rough sometimes, but do not go back! Stay Free!! If your path to your passion, purpose and power draws you away from a particular thing, stay on your path no matter what. Walk in your freedom, regardless of the difficulties that are associated with leaving "old things" behind. Remember, you can do *all things because Christ empowers you with inner strength; you are self-sufficient in Christ's sufficiency"* (Philippians 4:13 AMP). I used to interpret this scripture to mean that Christ was inside of me, doing powerful things through me. I have since realized that Christ is not the *doer,* I am. The power of God that raised Jesus Christ from the dead is not only available to me, but alive within me. My faith in the resurrection of Christ enjoins me to this power and equips me with the strength I need to do anything. And the same applies to every believer. Do not dwell on your limitations; dwell on your strength. Focus on the source of that strength – *God's power!* And with this power, you can do whatever it takes – no matter how frightful – to keep the liberty that has been imparted to your life. No one can walk in liberty for you; you must do that yourself. And, to go deeper, if you are not walking in the highest degree of liberty that you need to have a maximized life it is not God's failure, but your own. The quicker you learn the lesson, the faster you can turn your situation around. Learn that you deserve to be free, happy, peaceful, joyful, contented and fulfilled. And, according to your faith, you will be!

Stay Faithful

The late Rev. Hartman Guy Milton wrote a song that says, *"If you hold on, you can hold out. God will hold you up, if you remain faithful to Him."* These powerful lyrics offer an important key to living a life of power. In today's society, people have become accomplished at so many things. I often like to say, "We are a lot of things!" And yes we are. We are gifted. We are talented. We are popular. We are successful. And, we are charismatic. We are masters of slogans and chiefs of advertising. We are church connoisseurs, and we can plan conferences, workshops and retreats with the best of event organizers. Yes, we have many things underfoot; however, one thing is often missing from our personal constitution. Faithfulness. Another word for faithfulness is **consistency.** We must learn to be consistent with our life practices, and results will come. Sometimes, you can get so caught up in the *doing* of life, that you forget the *purpose* of *why* you are doing it. You render your gifts, talents, abilities and resources to various, noteworthy causes. And, in the pangs of "making it happen" the cost begins to overpower the *cause.* It becomes easy to forget that *to win it you've got to STAY IN IT!* You must stick with it and be consistent. You must be faithful. So, who qualifies as a "consistent" person? What do the "faithful" do? In a nutshell, they hang in there! They hold on until help comes. The faithful stay true to the cause even when the desired effect seems unlikely. Productive people remember that *"the race is not given to the swift, nor the battle to the strong but to him who remains in the end, the same shall be saved."*

I may be alone in my thinking, but I do not believe I am. As I said in the introduction of this book, I am ready to challenge traditional thinking that says the good times are just for the "by and by." I believe that faith and spirituality can have more than just a deferred positive impact on life. If your faith has indeed given you salvation, be saved in every aspect of your life. Be saved from defeat! Saved from fear! Saved from self-destructive behaviors! Saved from procrastination! Saved from outside attacks! Saved from ulterior motives! Saved from tradition! Saved! Saved! Saved! And because most things take time and involve lengthy processes, be saved from quitting. Anticipate that things will not always be easy. But that does not matter, because you have been given the knowledge and the tools to always win! Just stick with it and be consistent. Remove quitting, giving up, failure, and excuses from your vocabulary. Set your eyes on your future and your promise, and move forward.

Again, this is not to say that you will always experience life as a bed of roses. To the contrary, many times you fall into traps, trials and situations that seem to contradict your faith confessions. However, you must know which strategy to employ in order to access victory through the power that is available to you. Recently, I heard this statement, *"There are two types of people in the world:* **believers and unbelievers.** *The only difference is that believers know who to complain to."* I would like to exchange the words *consistent* and *inconsistent,* so that the statement says, *"There are two types of people in the world – the consistent and the inconsistent!"* The consistent are faced with the same challenges as the inconsistent. They do not get a pass to easy street, just because they aspire to do great things. However, when you are a consistent person, you understand that lofty aspirations are not tickets of escape. Neither is faith a predictor – or dictator – of the future. On the contrary, faith does not dictate what happens in life. Rather, faith determines how consistent people respond to the things that happen.

You might see these statements as contradictory to the teaching that a person's faith can produce the life he or she may desire. From our limited, human understanding, there can appear to be insurmountable paradoxes to a life lived by faith. For example, if God is in control of everything and if your times are indeed in the hands of God, who gets the credit when things are in turmoil? Since God gets credit when things are going well, who is to blame when things are going poorly? The devil? That seems to contradict the belief that God is always in control. But there is no contradiction at all, because the issue is not one of polarized authorities. The real issue is a matter of individual consistency. What you do in the face of trouble and adversity is your choice. The results that your choices yield in your life are your doing. To be faithfully consistent and to perform at optimal levels, you must trust that your steps are ordered, even when the path leads you through seasons of testing, persevering and yes – *waiting!* If you give up once you have started, then you might as well have never started at all.

> *Psalm 77:2-3, "In the day of my trouble I sought the Lord;*
> *my hand was stretched out in the night without ceasing;*
> *My soul refused to be comforted. I remembered God."*

In order to walk in the power that allows you to do any and everything, you must remain faithful and consistent even when you walk through situations that turn your life upside down. When your soul cannot be calmed or comforted, continue to do what you have always done. Have faith. Even when having faith appears not to produce the results promised. Do not give up! Come to the conclusion that the circumstances of your life will not dictate what you believe or what you hope for. Know that you can even get angry and ask the questions *"Why me?" "What did I do to deserve this?"* Give yourself the miracle of the answer *"I don't know"* whenever you need to. To say, *"I don't know"* does not mean that you do not have faith. On the contrary, it means that even when your faith seems to contradict your existence you will not let it go. You will admit the facts, but the facts do not change your truth.

You have been given gifts, talents, abilities, skills, and experiences that can bring about positive change in people's lives. When you allow yourself to be empowered and strengthened, you render a performance worthy of a standing ovation. That is the real meaning of what it is to have lived – *that you made a difference.* The light of your life process ignites the light in someone else's life and shines forever. What is in you that can change the world one person at a time? Are you ready? Lights! Camera! Action! *You're on!*

Principle #6 – Prevailing
Winning at the Game of Life

How do you determine when you have achieved success? How do you know when you are on the right path? How can you tell if your team is winning? The answer can be put this way – *follow the plan and purpose that is specifically designed for you, and you will always win.* To prevail essentially means to win. In order for this to be your life's experience your must be driven by purpose in all of your motives and actions. Success (another word for winning) is a relative and subjective term. In other words, when you get to the point where you determine what is successful for you, you have truly obtained a life that is powerful, meaningful and rewarding. When all is said and done, it must be *your life's plan* that takes priority for you over everything else.

> *Romans 8:27-28 reads, "Now He who searches the hearts knows what the mind of the Spirit is, because He makes intercession for the saints according to the will of God. And we know that all things work together for good to those who love God, to those who are the called according to His purpose."*

Another translation reads, *"That's why we can be so sure that every detail of our lives of love for God is worked into something good."*

The word purpose is both a noun and a verb. As a verb it means to will, to have deliberate intention, to take counsel with oneself, and to determine with oneself. In the noun form – the word becomes "prosthesis" – "pro" means before and "thesis" means a place. Thus, a purpose is something has been settled before. The word suggests a deliberate plan, a proposition, an advanced plan, an intention and a design. So, for people seeking a life of power and purpose this means understanding that a deliberated, advanced plan for your life was established and settled before your life began.

Therefore, even when the journey seems uncertain, you can trust that something wonderful is unfolding every day of your life. That something is your purpose. And when you are looking for ways to win in life the best strategy is to seek out your ultimate, divine purpose first, and then allow everything else to fall in line accordingly. Winning starts with the recognition of and submission to the truth that a higher agenda has been set. The process of life includes the lessons that are learned as sojourners embark upon the process of realizing goals and objectives. And "life champions" become experts in understanding that the goals and objectives for a person's life are not the things that lie outside of it. Rather, they come from deep within and are discovered as you learn more about yourself, who you really are, and what you truly want.

Remember, success is relative and subjective. What can be called success for one might not be success for another. What one person makes look easy, might wear another person out within twenty-four hours. To win you must know what winning feels like *for you.* And that is not something that you can learn from a motivational message, seminar or workshop. To know what winning is and to know how to win in life comes from an inner peace that is realized through the recognition of the awesomely divine presence that is within everyone.

How to Prevail All of the Time

There is a way of thinking that can promise that you do not have to have another down day in your life. This is not to say that circumstances and situations will not arise that merit feeling badly or even sorry about. However, you must remember that the path for success has already been designed for you and that life is the process of learning and unlearning the necessary lessons to reveal that path. Then, you must develop a healthy mentality that allows you to see the bright side of all circumstances. This is not easy and doing so requires a lot of prayer, meditation, strength of character and determination. You might feel as if you are in a paradoxical existence, somewhere between **standing** and **striving.** While you use the strategies and principles learned to stand in confidence and manage your present, you must also actively engage these same ideas to strive for your future. It can be a place of conflict, because you know that where you are is good, but there is better to be had. Furthermore, although it is not easy to be in this place, wise people do not try to avoid here because they understand it to be crucial for their growth and development. In this place – the space between standing and striving – you learn crucial lessons that build your character. Character is a very important attribute, because having character will allow you to handle the great things that are in store for you. So then, striving is the process that pushes you forward and moves you towards your destiny. Standing is the ability to seize the day and be happy where you are. You are content enough to be happy with what you have, while at the same time forging full force ahead to what you believe you can obtain. When you master this mind set, you win all of the time. You are able to think futuristically without become frustrated. You practice being content but not contrary; constrained but not complacent. The place between standing and striving is a tedious place and many successful people make it appear easy or perhaps even non-existent. However, it is not and effectively dealing with everyday life while looking for a brighter day is a skill you will use forever, because there are always higher heights and deeper depths. There is always more you can do with your life. Do not allow yourself to become stuck. Rather than be stuck, multi-task! Stand and strive! Strive and stand! You are indeed a winner!

Prevail Over People

When you seek to live a life of power, passion and purpose, people can get in your way. Human beings are relational creatures, and in most instances they are utterly loyal to their relationships. This is one of the finer, more redemptive qualities of the human race. Unfortunately, it can also be a virtue that can work against you if not channeled properly. Referring again to the issues of proper boundaries and parameters, people are often loyal whether the relationships are healthy or unhealthy. But again, if you are going to prevail, you must not let any relationship get in your way. This also means learning the lesson of getting over the opinion of others.

Imagine you lived in a time where men could legally be married to as many women as they could provide for. Your husband has several wives. Of all his wives, you are his favorite and the other wives hate you for it. One of them in particular sees you as her primary rival and archenemy. She taunts you because she can give your husband a child and you cannot. You know in your heart that a part of your life's purpose is to bear a child of purpose. But in order to see that day manifest, you have to live through some really difficult times. Being misunderstood, ostracized and mocked are everyday norms for you. One day, a respect religious leader in your community accuses you of being obsessed and delusional because you so desperately want to have a baby. But even through all of this you stand strong and eventually give birth to your destiny. What a dynamic example of someone prevailing over people. This is exactly what Hannah, a famous biblical character, went through. Even though the odds were stacked against her, Hannah was relentless. She saw herself giving birth to a child – a male child – who would grow up and have a significant impact on her people's history. Being an Israelite, she believed that God had ordained this for her. And she was determined to be successful, regardless of what people thought. Her determination and persistence eventually led to the prophet Elijah giving her a declaration of confirmation that she would indeed prevail over seemingly impossible circumstances. This Elijah was the same prophet who had accused her of being drunk while she prayed at the wall. She gave birth to Samuel, a powerful man who became a judge, priest and might figure in Israel. However, as powerful as his life turned out to be, none if it would have happened if Hannah had not prevailed over her hellish experience. What might have happened if she had been more concerned with how people felt about her? What might have become of her dream of being a mother? What would have happened to her desire to render a child to be used for power, passion and purpose? How would Israel's history have been changed, if Samuel had not lived to impact it? Gratefully, we will never have to answer these questions, because Hannah prevailed. In spite of people, Hannah won. She encountered difficulties, but she overcame them because she tapped into her divine ability to create her future.

Perhaps your life is filled with challenge. Maybe you feel as if you have never been given a fair chance. Peradventure you come from a dysfunctional family, a single parent home, or an abusive background. You may be more like Hannah than you care to admit. But in the end, Hannah had the last laugh, and so can you. If you are going to prevail, you must get over the opinion of others. Look again at Hannah as an example. She stood at that wall rocking back and forth, pleading her case to God, even though it appeared to others that she was drunk. Even a very prestigious religious leader from her community thought that Hannah was under the influence of alcohol. However, Hannah did not care. In her eyes, part of her divine purpose was to bear a child – a male child – that she would offer back to the Lord in service. And, she was determined to have an audience with God, even though the people around her did not understand. Her determination and persistence not only got the attention of Elijah, but he also gave her a very promising word about her future. That promise led to a son named Samuel. Samuel became the founder of Israel's prophetic ministry as an institution. Samuel was also a judge and a priest, and a mighty figure in the history of Israel. And, as powerful as Samuel's life turned out to be, you cannot forget that none of it would have happened if Hannah had not prevailed over her hellish circumstances.

> *Psalm 126, versus 5 and 6 says, "Those who sow in tears shall reap in joy. He who continually goes forth weeping, bearing seed for sowing, shall doubtless come again with rejoicing, bringing his sheaves (the harvest) with him."*

What a promise! You are not only promised total restoration from sorrow and tears, but you have also been given a promise – *a guaranteed promise* – of a harvest to follow. In other words, in the end you win and you will also get prizes. Nevertheless, if you give in to the pressure and fail to continue in sowing, even through your tears, you will lose out on your promise. Ask yourself the same question that we asked about Samuel and Israel. What about the people who are destined to cross paths with you and never be the same again? What about the precious things you can teach them? In order to find out, make up your mind that you will prevail over the people who in any way oppose your success.

Prevail Over Pride

I believe that pride is a castle that the mind erects to protect itself against the devastation caused by failure. It camouflages itself in many disguises, such as over-achieving, perfectionism, criticism and even apathy. But the true culprit in these instances is pride nonetheless; a house of cards that will tumble to the ground if confronted. So, in order to deal with pride, you must address your thoughts and how they are constructed. Mastering the mind is crucial to prevailing over pride. For the mind is where pride takes up residence and makes itself at home.

Your mind tells you stories about your life that seem very real and true. Your mind can look at a glass and see it as either half empty or half full. Your mind determines whether or not a broken down car is a sign of blessing or a curse. Your mind begins to compare you with other people and then tells you that somehow you do not measure up to some obscure standard. What you often do not realize is that even the standard itself is a creation of the mind and the only person who can give you a passing grade is you. This same mind tells you that you do not have a problem and there is no need for help. Therefore, you go on for years feeling empty and depleted without ever seeking out spiritual or personal guidance. And, at the root of it all is pride. To conquer pride is to move that much closer to being the winner you were destined to be.

Prevailing over pride requires clarity about who is important and what truly matters. In the chapter on *Performing,* I discussed being detached from your output. This means that you do not determine your value based on what you do. On the contrary, knowing who you are and what you are sent here to do enables you to perform to the highest degree possible for you. You are not competing with anyone. You can win the victory over pride by focusing on the one person who truly counts. Your mission is to please an audience of one – *the God in you.*

Proud people are too good for trouble. Proud people feel they have been too faithful for trials and tribulations. Proud people are overly concerned with what other people think. Do not fall victim to this defeated mentality. Prevail over the spirit of pride, so that your purpose and passion can produce real power in your life. Do not worry about where your pride says you should be. Do not concern yourself with what your pride says you should have accomplished by now. Do not fret over the things that pride says you should possess. Use the powerful principles in this book and others you have learned to win out over pride. Always remember that pride is a tedious and persistent foe. Pride will creep in when you least expect it. Remind yourself that pride can disguise itself as ambition, initiative and assertiveness. You must be clever and clear to make the distinction and to discern whether you are being motivated by a healthy sense of self or an unhealthy presence of pride. One way to tell the difference is to evaluate your response to the unexpected. Your level of peace, even when dealing with undesirable situations, is an indicator of whether you are winning over pride. Remember that pride and peace cannot coexist; they are archenemies of one another. If the unexpected embarrasses you and makes you quit, then your pride wins. If the appearance of delays upsets you, then your pride has pulled out in front of you and is racing towards the finish line. But you can overcome the pitfalls of fear and pride. Every plan has a timeline and unexpected circumstances will not have to derail your progress forever. Develop the winning attitude that you will go with the flow and trust everything to work out as it should.

> *Let patience have her perfect work, that you may be perfect and complete, wanting nothing (James 1:4)*

> *But as for me, I trust in You, O Lord. I say you are my God. For my times are in your hand. (Psalm 31:14 & 15)*

> *The end of a thing is better than the beginning of a thing and patience is better than price. (Ecclesiastes 7:8)*

Resolve to trust the process. Humble yourself and participate in the journey, even when you cannot dictate the details. Allow your trials, tests, and unexpected setbacks to teach you valuable lessons, but not to define your value. Remember you are already a winner and an overcomer. Prevail and move forward! Your destiny is waiting.

Prevail Over Pain

Heartache is another often overlooked obstacle to success. Pain can block your view of your purpose as you proceed on your journey. As you move towards a life of power, there will be times of pain. There will be spiritual pain, emotional pain, and psychological pain. Sometimes you can hurt so badly, you will forget all about your dreams. Survival becomes your main and only objective. Finding the strength to merely get out of bed; go to work, and continue in your various roles is the most you can give. The promises, dreams and plans that once motivated you to move forward are now figments of your imagination, mere signs of who you once dreamed you could be. Pain can keep you from moving forward, leaving you stuck on **Self Pity Street** or **Woe is Me Avenue.** Pain can become a permanent resident in your mind that you become so accustomed to, you forget what life was like without it. Nevertheless, even when pain seems to be the order of the day, you must trust that everything you have experienced can be used for some good. You must believe that you have the power, strength, intellect, wit and determination to still make your dreams happen. Like the old commercial for Ragu spaghetti sauce used to say, *"It's in there!"* What you need to win is inside of you. Refuse to be stopped, no matter what happens. Do not lose your faith in God or your confidence in yourself, because you encounter seasons of pain.

I am sure that you have come through many trials. In your life, you have overcome seemingly unbeatable odds that were stacked against you. Out of these experiences comes a resolve to prevail over every opposing factor that might keep you from reaching your goals and realizing your dreams. But that is not always the case. Sometimes the pain appears larger than your resolve. There is a lot of personal work that must be done by you in order to reach a place where you are winning even over pain. Pain is no laughing matter. The issue of pain should not be dismissed with slogans or colloquialisms. Therefore, I am a strong proponent of the counseling and self-reflection that usually must be done, in order for true healing to take place. This does not mean that God cannot heal your heart and mind at the snap of His finger. On the contrary, I believe that the two work together. I dare say that if you are not committed to doing the work, then you will restrict your level of success and limit the manifestation of true power in your life.

Here are a few strategies for dealing with pain that I've learned and recommend to you.

1. Keep things in perspective.
2. Forgive quickly.

3. Love unconditionally.
4. Think positively.
5. Live authentically.
6. Allow others to help.
7. Act decisively.

Get Life! Get Power! Get LifePOWER!

For More Help and Information with living a life of power

Attend a LifePOWER workshop!

LifePOWER is series of life-coaching resources, including LifePOWER the book, the LifePOWER Impact Sessions & Workshops, and one-on-one LifePOWER mentoring with Co-Pastor Veda.

The LifePOWER Impact Session is a non-traditional venue where people come for real talk about real issues to get real results that lead to real POWER for REAL LIVING. It covers a myriad of areas -- spiritual, emotional, psychological, intellectual and personal development. LifePOWER principles explore self improvement through coaching, employing best practices, self-reflection and networking.

For more information on LifePOWER, visit Veda McCoy's website at www.veda.mccoy.com/lifepower today!

Get Your Copy of Co-Pastor Veda's Next Book

"Children Don't Come from The Grocery Store!"

Release Date – Spring 2010

Other Life Changing Products
by
Co-Pastor Veda McCoy

- Look At This Woman (Book & Sermon)

- Children Don't Come from the Grocery Store (Book)

- Spiritual Warfare in a Contemporary Society (Audio Series & Bible Study Guide)

- Keys to Financial Health & Wealth (Bible Study Guide)

- Warrior Disciples Who Win (Audio Series & Bible Study Guide)

- Vision (Sermon Series)

- A New Thing (Sermon Series)

- *And many more!*

To order these and other products, or to invite Veda McCoy to your area, visit www.vedamccoy.com.

About the Author

Veda McCoy is a dynamic and influential woman, who motivates and inspires thousands of people worldwide. A powerful speaker, teacher, co-pastor and vocalist, Veda McCoy assists her husband, Senior Pastor Marvin E. McCoy, at Judah Christian Center Church in Suitland, Maryland, a fast-growing ministry committed to empowering people and changing lives. They are the proud parents of two adult children, Marvin Myer and Johntae Marvyce.

Veda McCoy uses biblical principles to elevate people from mediocrity to greatness, as they strive to live their best lives. She is widely known for her life-changing speaking, teaching, prophetic insight, and empowering events. Her debut book *Look At This Woman: Destroying the Bondage of Low Self-Esteem,* has helped many to improve their lives. In addition to being a published author, Veda McCoy has released three music projects, *Reality (1993); Over Again (1996); and Renewed Strength ~ Live in Washington, DC (1999).* She was also a featured soloist on Pastor Shirley Caesar's 1997 release *A Miracle in Harlem,* on the selection "So Satisfied."

Veda McCoy is committed to helping ordinary people – particularly women – lead extraordinary lives. Every summer, people travel nationwide to attend her **"Annual Old Fashioned Prayer Breakfast."** This annual event stirs up the gift and power of prayer in the lives of attendees and reignites their passion for on-going, intimate fellowship with God. Veda McCoy also leads several initiatives that encourage personal growth, provide mentorship, cultivate ideas and talents, and inspire people to dream and revitalize their lives. A few include, **Sisters of The Light,** a mentoring program for women and young girls; **Finding Elizabeth Mentoring Program,** a complete mentoring curriculum, **Sisters With Things in Common,** a fellowship for women leaders, and **LifePOWER,** a book and series of life-coaching workshops for everyone.

In addition to being a spiritual leader, pastor and life coach, Veda McCoy is also a passionate educator. She holds a Bachelor of Arts degree in English from Bowie State University, (where she graduated *Magna cum laude)*, a Master of Theological Studies degree from Wesley Theological Seminary, and is also a certified English teacher in the state of Maryland. Currently she is pursuing a graduate degree in Educational School Administration and Supervision and plans to later obtain a doctoral degree in Organizational Leadership. A proven and successful reading specialist, Veda McCoy is also workshop presenter and staff development consultant. She developed ***Strategies for Academic Success and Scholarship***, a workshop for parents desiring to ensure high level of academic achievement and college preparation for their children.

Veda McCoy desires to see people empowered to live victoriously and abundantly, free to pursue passion, fulfill destiny and realize dreams. A life sacrificed to personal development and public service, her motto is *"For though I be free from all men, yet have I made myself servant unto all, that I might gain the more."*